Welcome to a realm where the boundaries of conventional aesthetics are shattered, and the juxtaposition of the extraordinary and the ethereal becomes a canvas of boundless imagination. "Monstrous Embrace" beckons you to journey beyond the realms of familiarity and delve into a world where the grotesque and the graceful coalesce in unexpected harmony.

Within these pages, witness an array of captivating images that transcend mere appearances, portraying monstrous beings intertwined with women of diverse origins. This audacious exploration of contrasts challenges societal norms and invites contemplation on the essence of attraction, acceptance, and the myriad facets of beauty. "Monstrous Embrace" is more than just a collection of striking visuals——it is a celebration of the intricacies of human connection and the enchanting dance between the known and the mysterious.

Embark on a voyage of self-discovery as you absorb the stories woven between these extraordinary pairings. Each image encapsulates a narrative of companionship that defies the mundane and fosters a deeper understanding of what it means to truly connect. As you turn the pages, allow your perceptions to expand and your heart to embrace the unexpected. "Monstrous Embrace" invites you to reevaluate the definitions of allure and repulsion, prompting introspection and leaving an indelible mark on your soul.

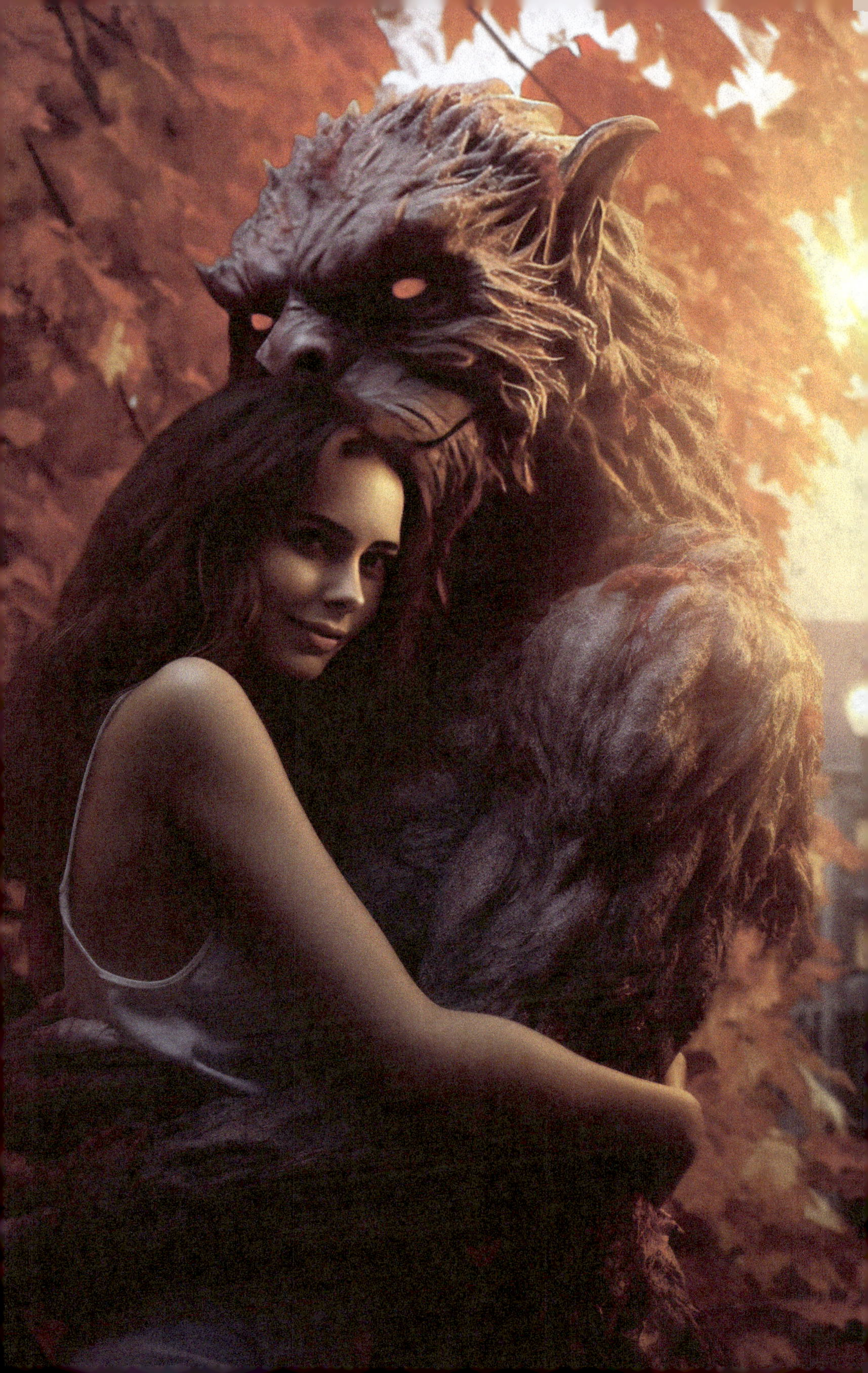

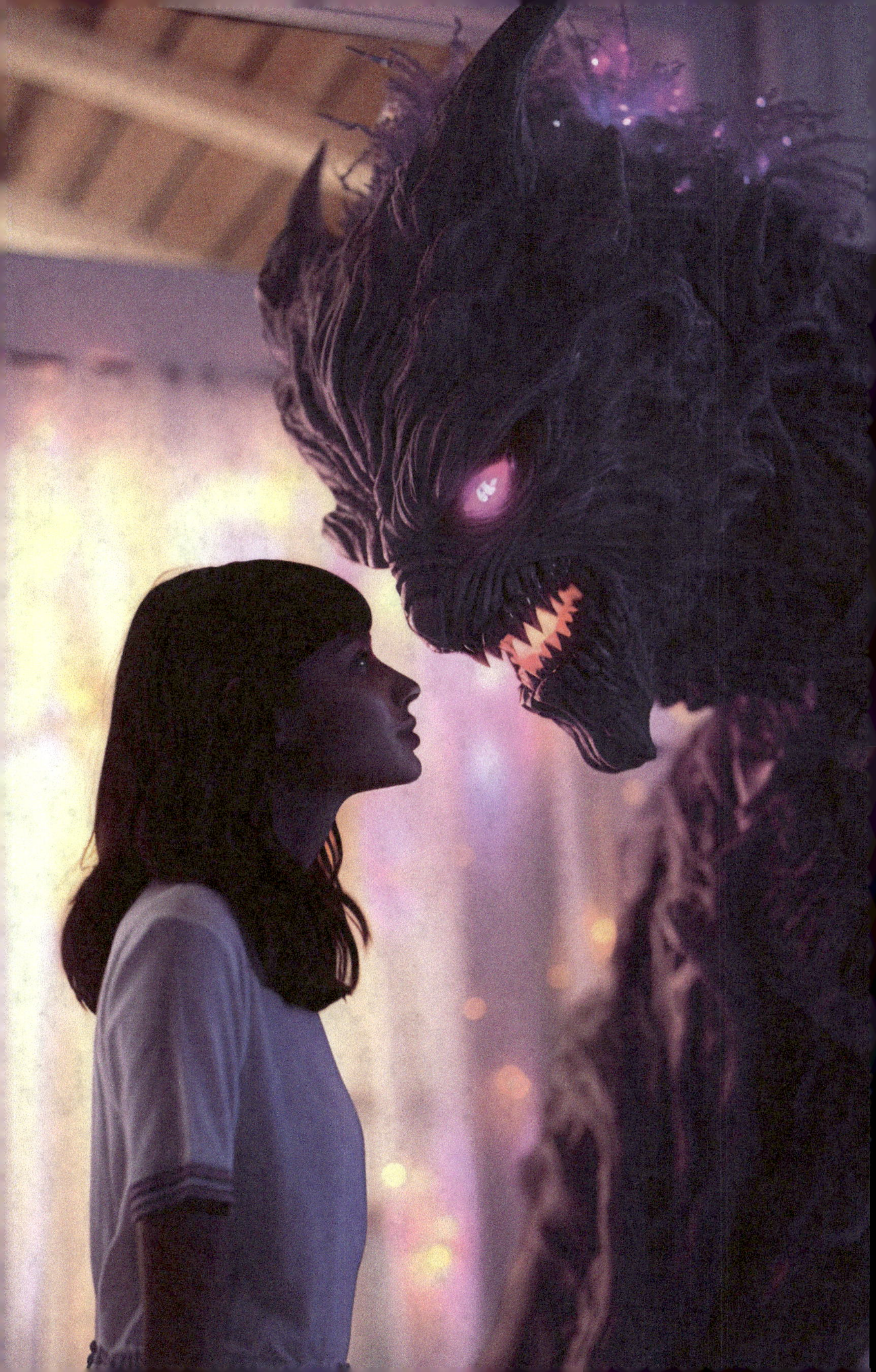

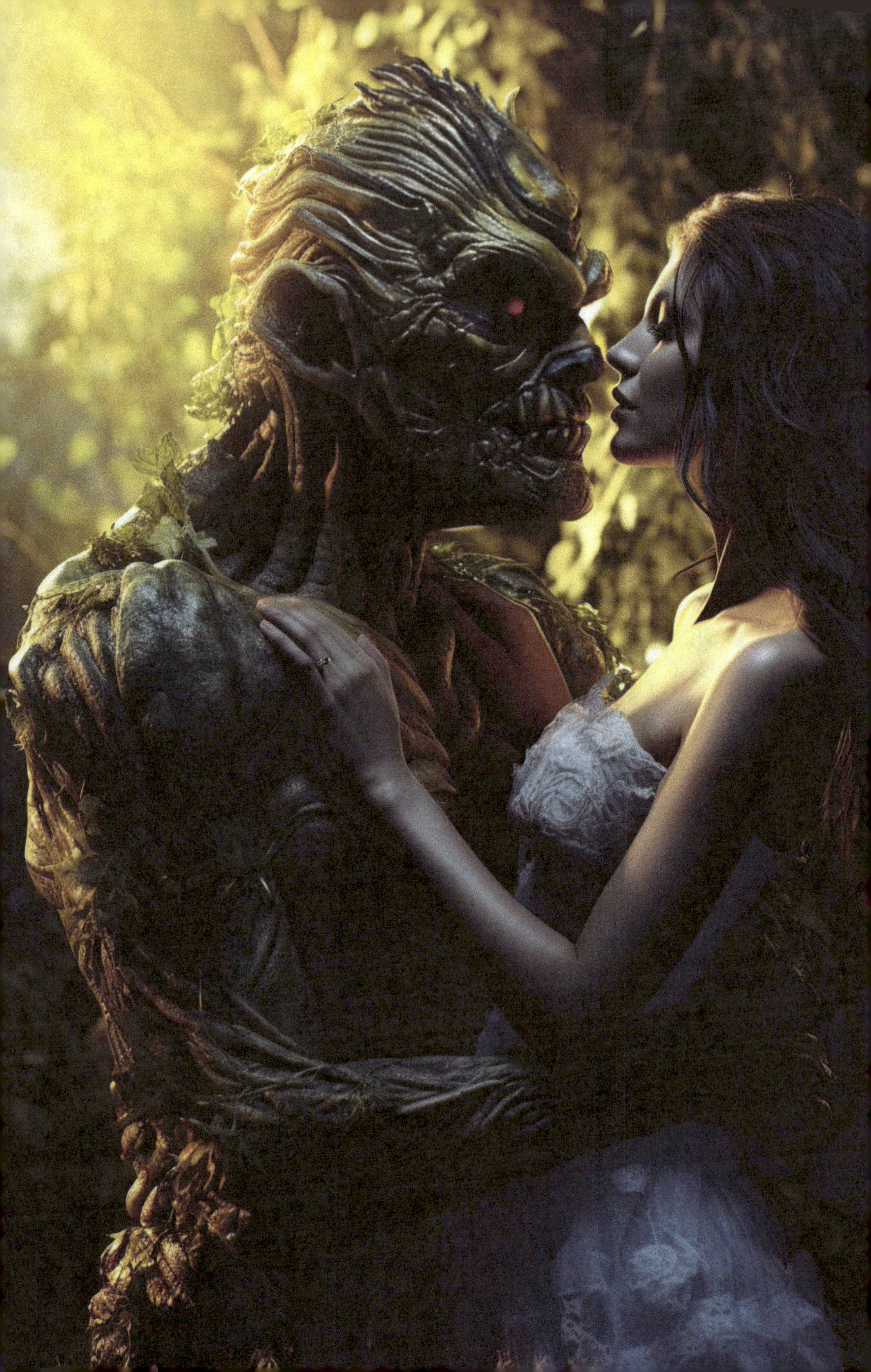

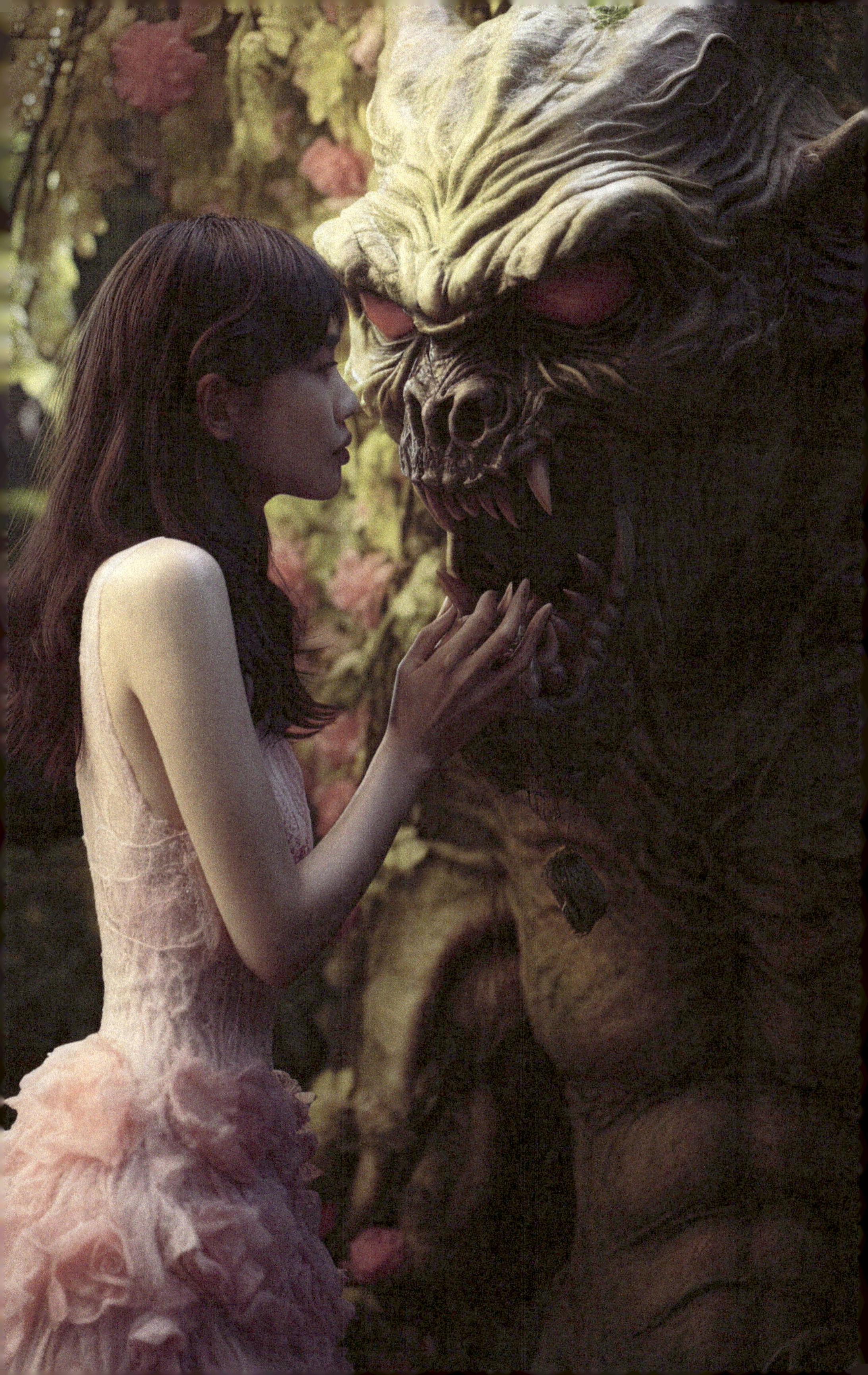

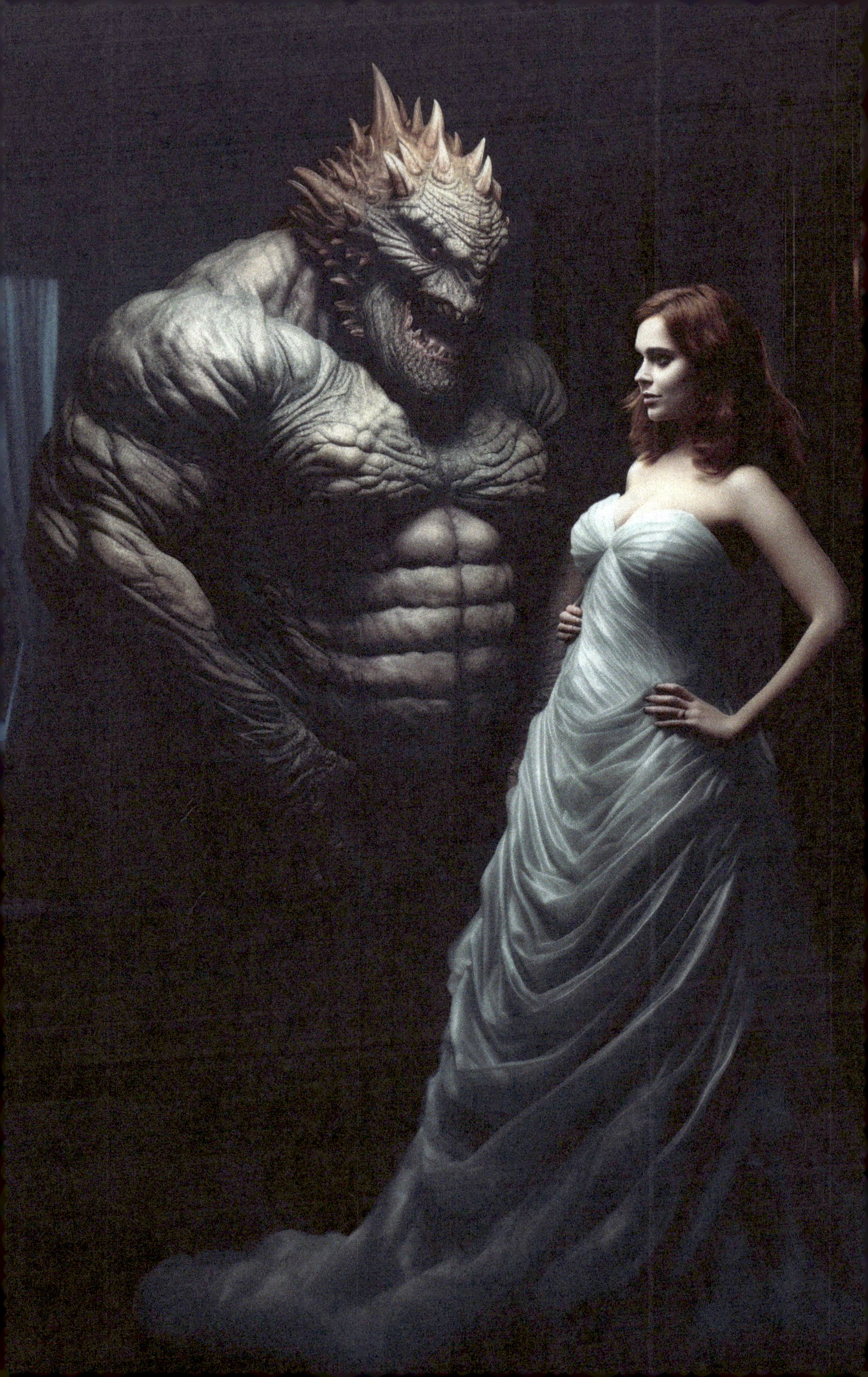

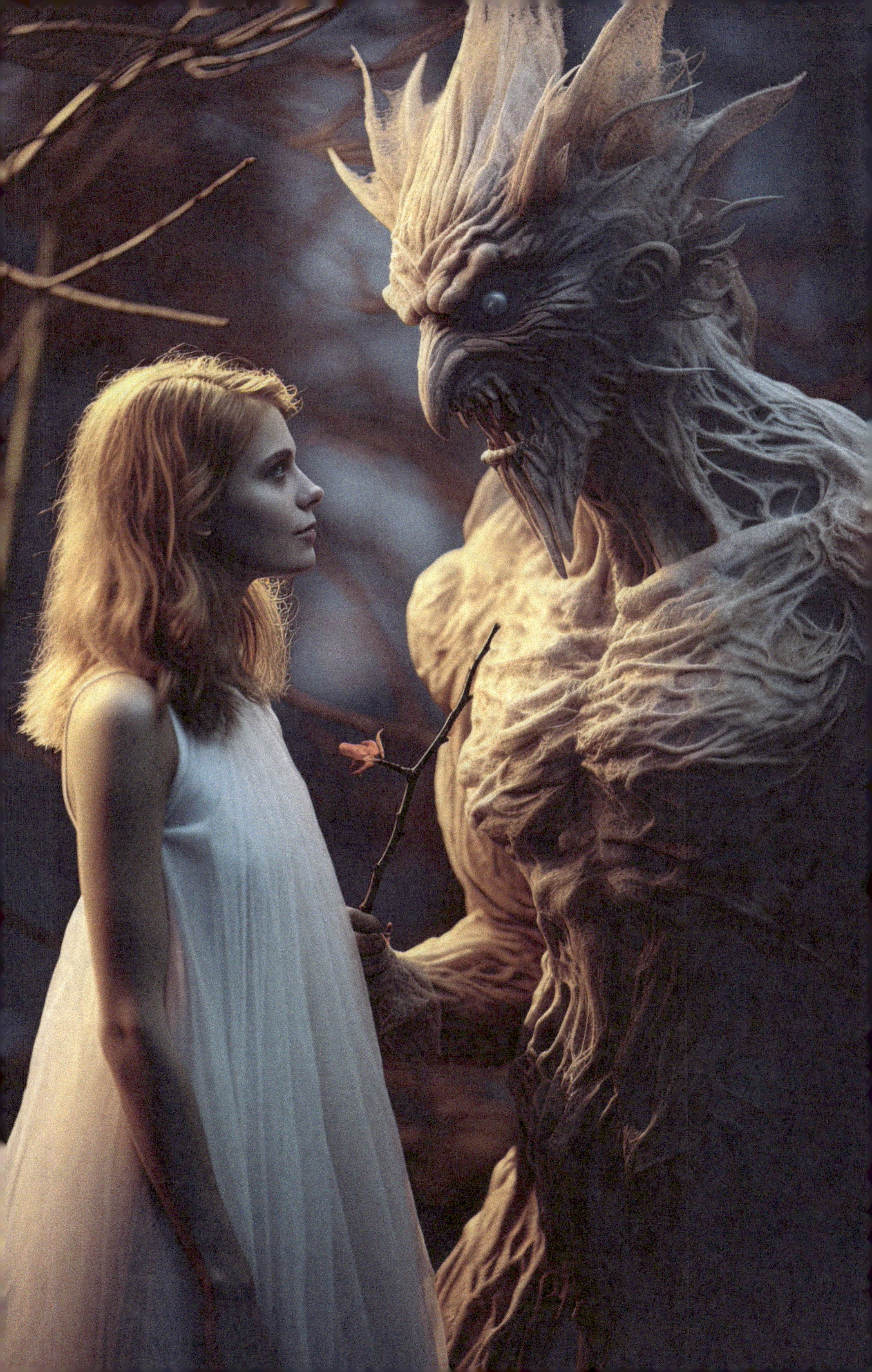

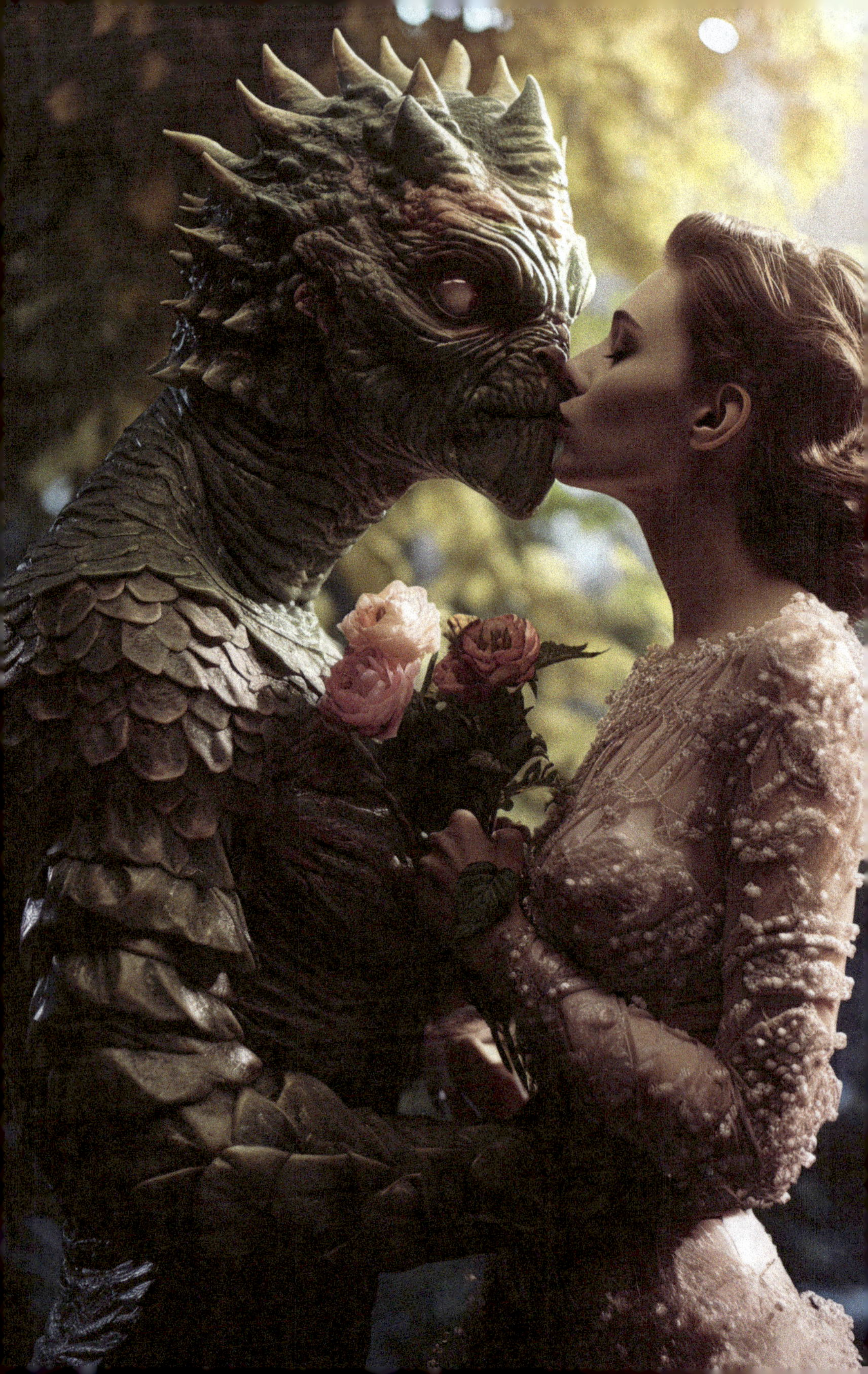

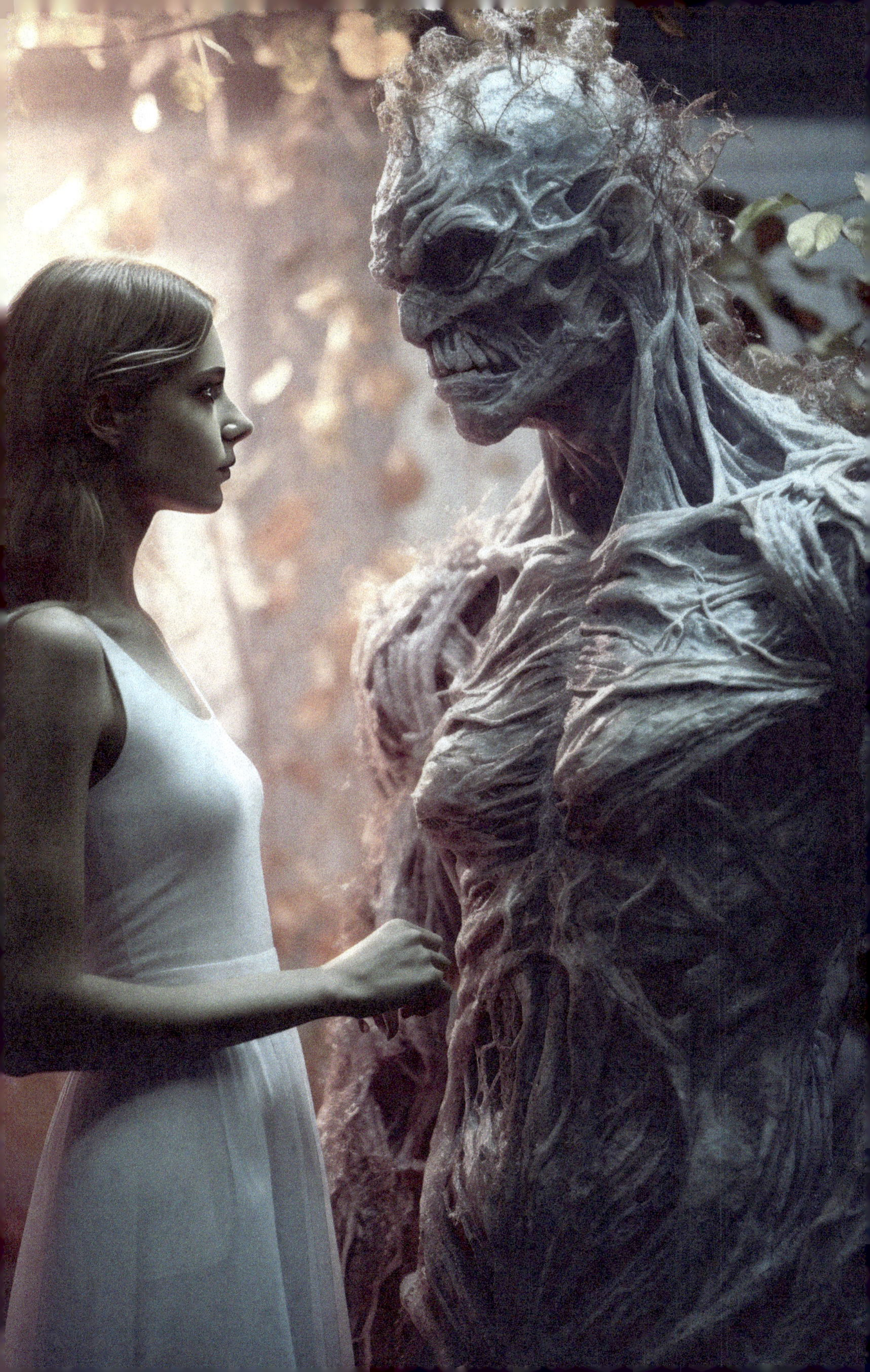

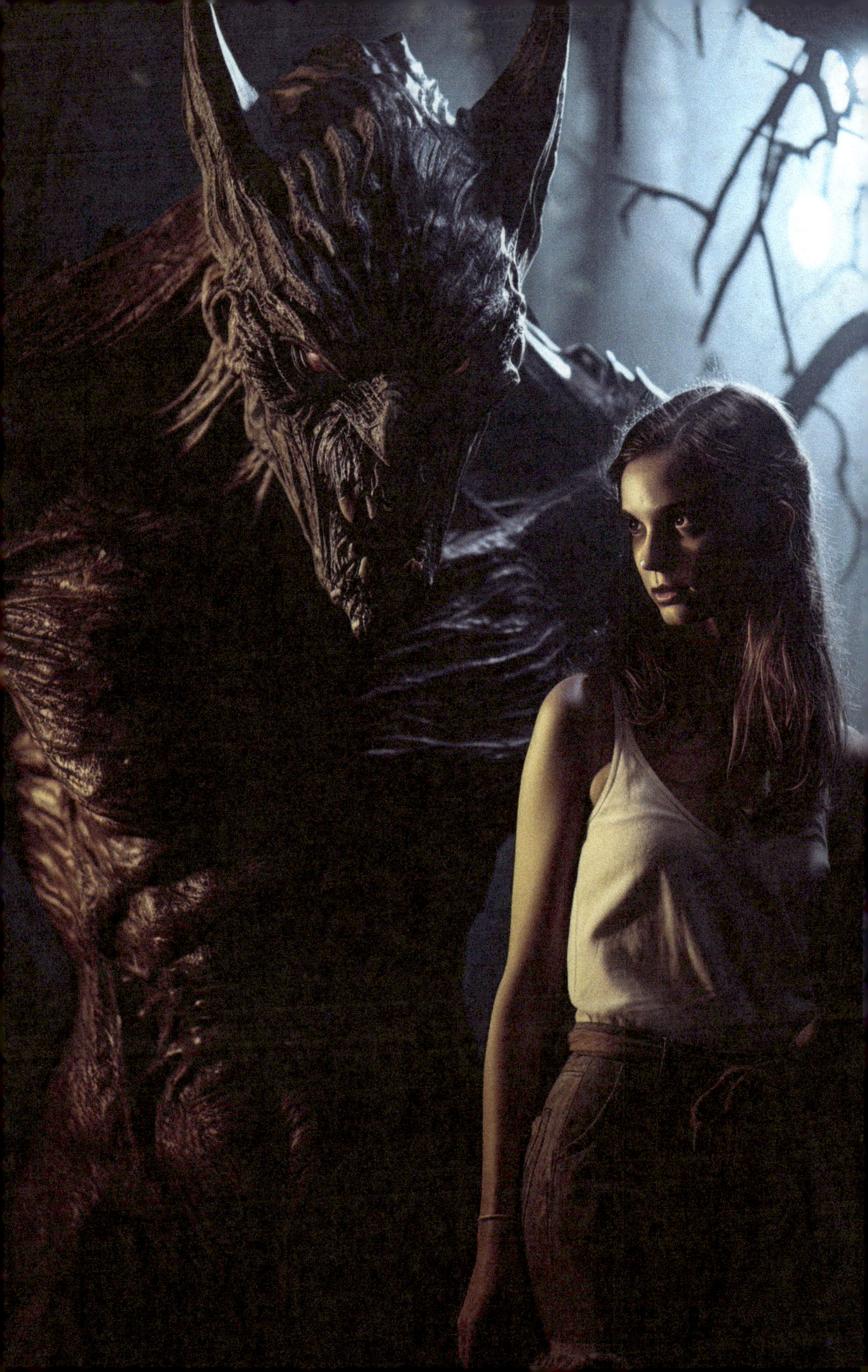

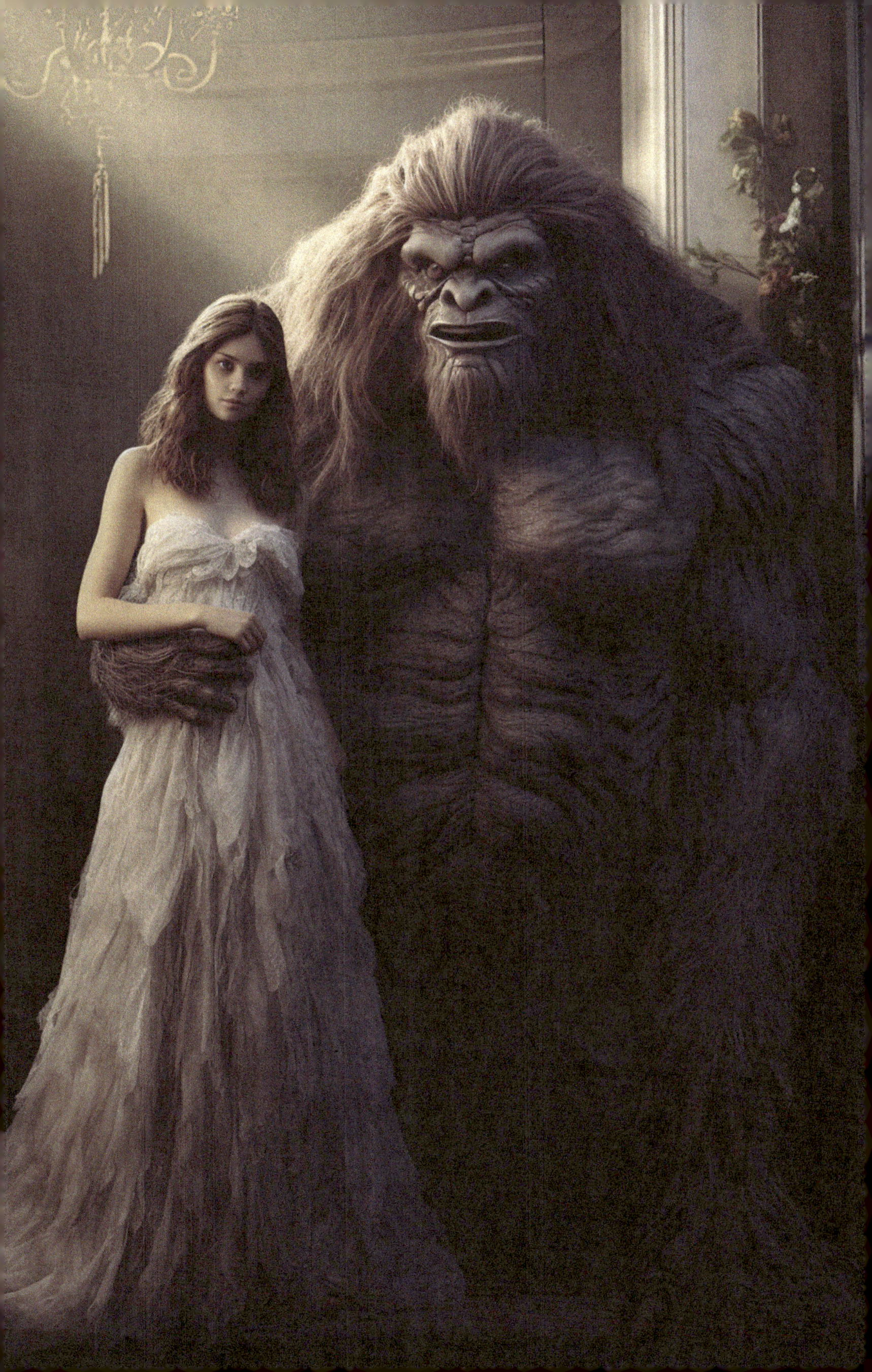

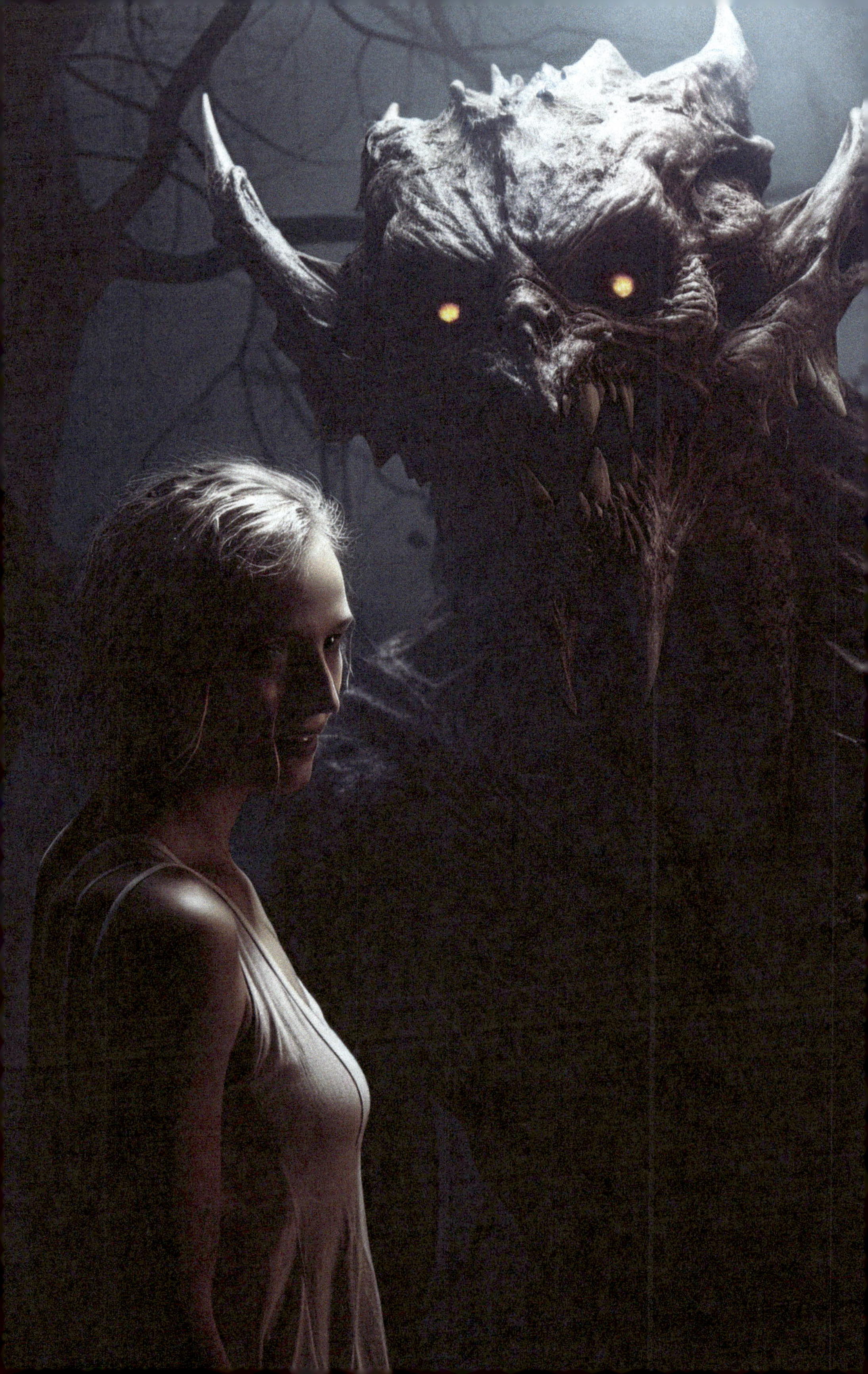

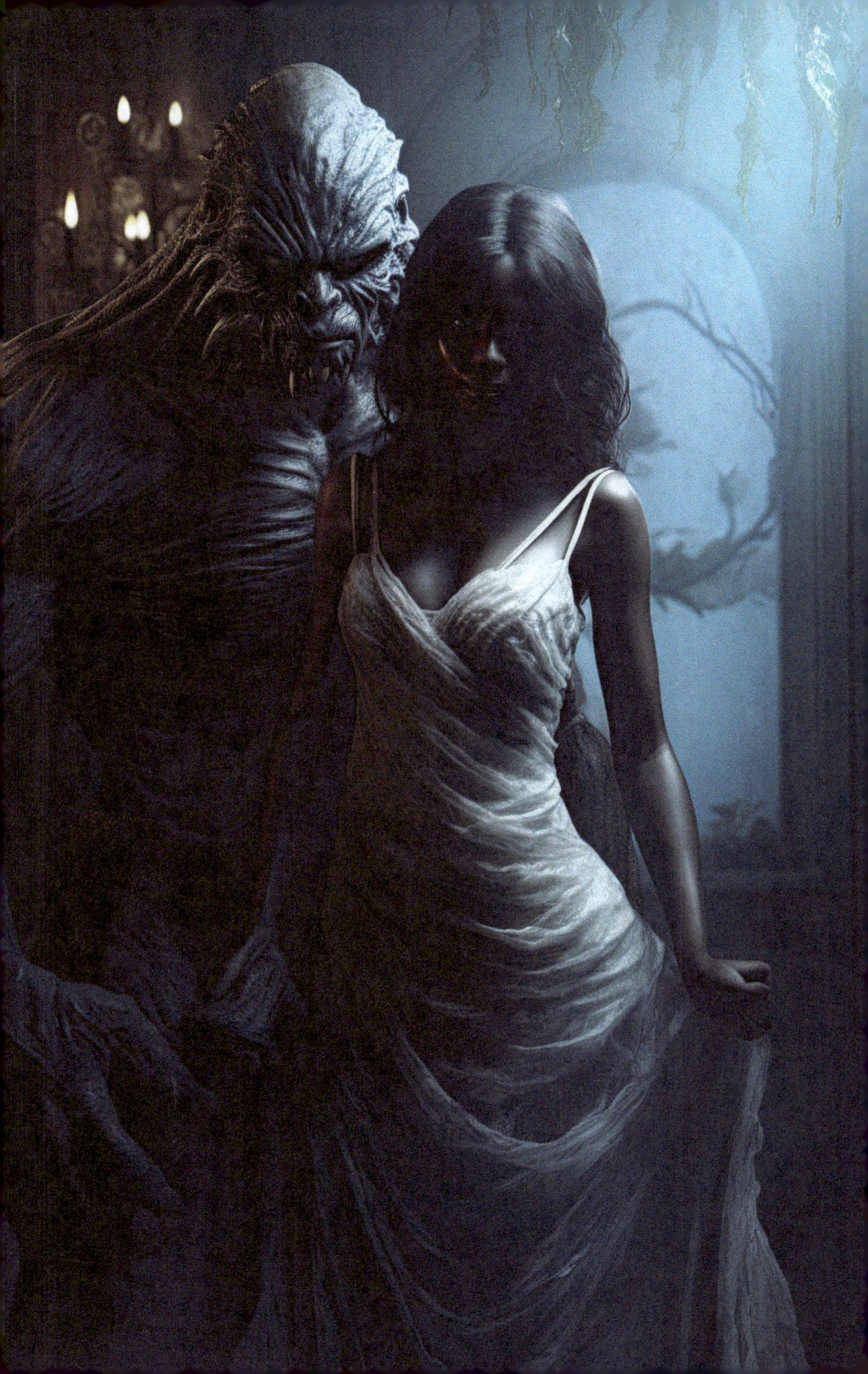

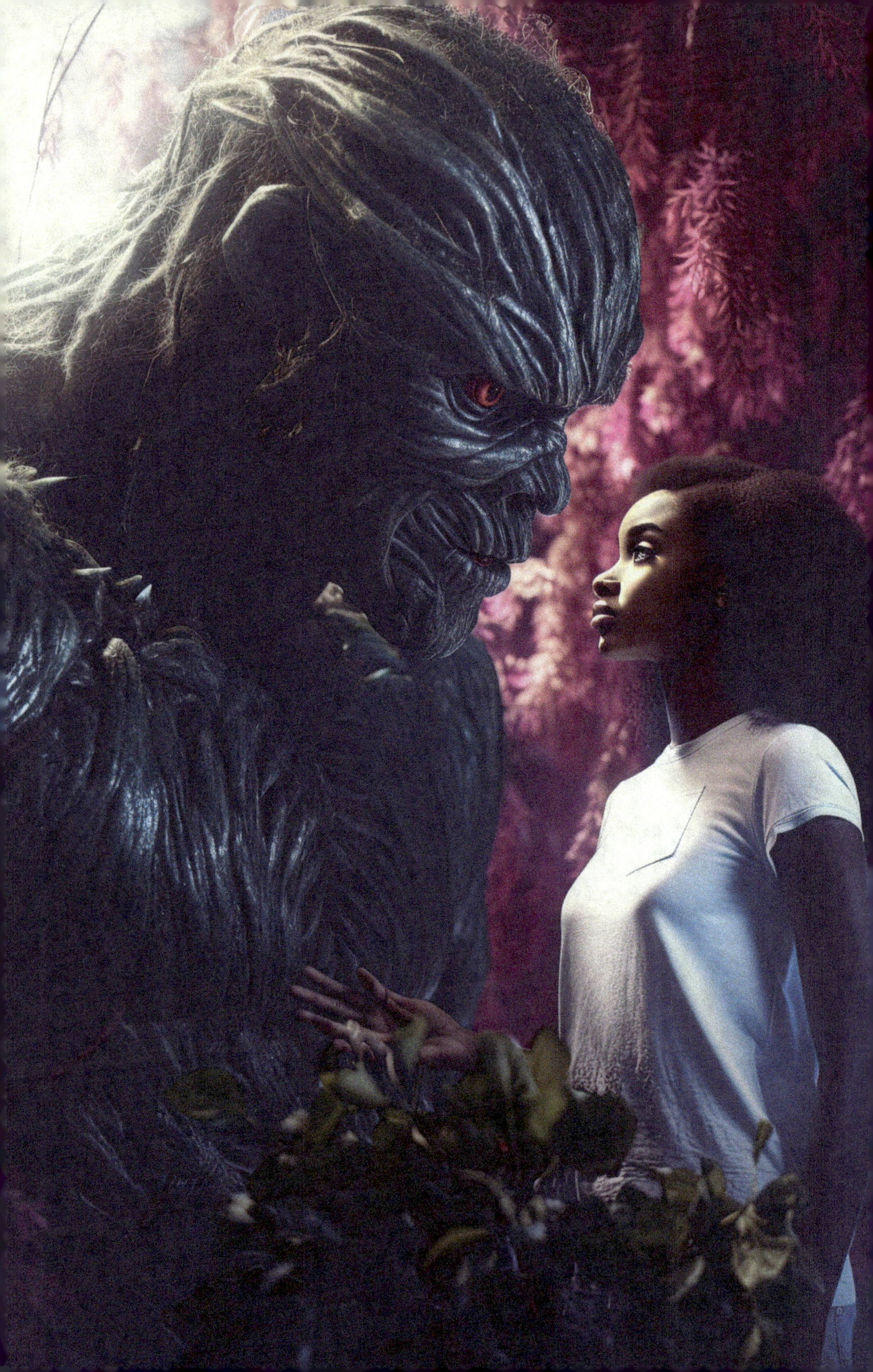

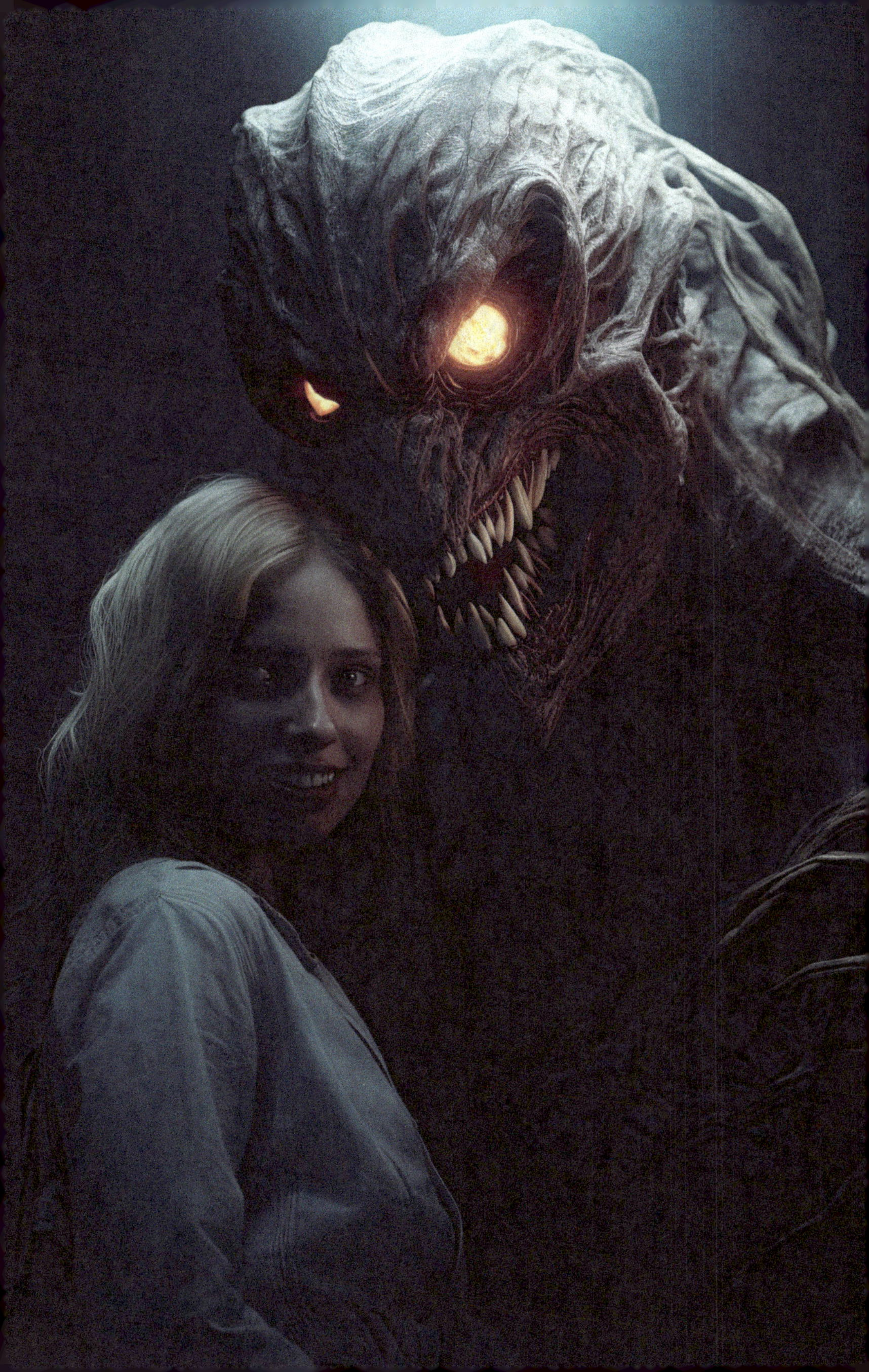

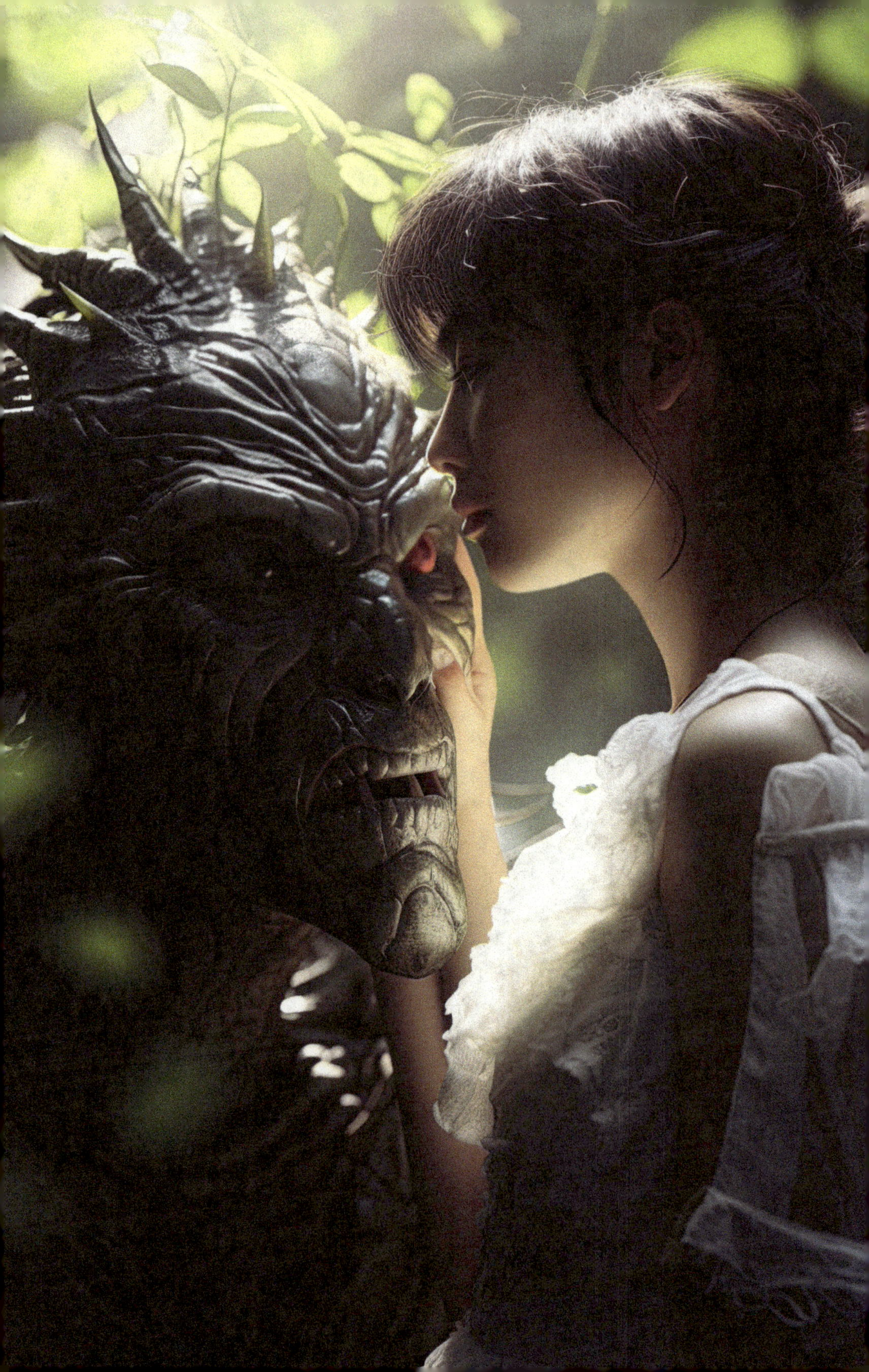

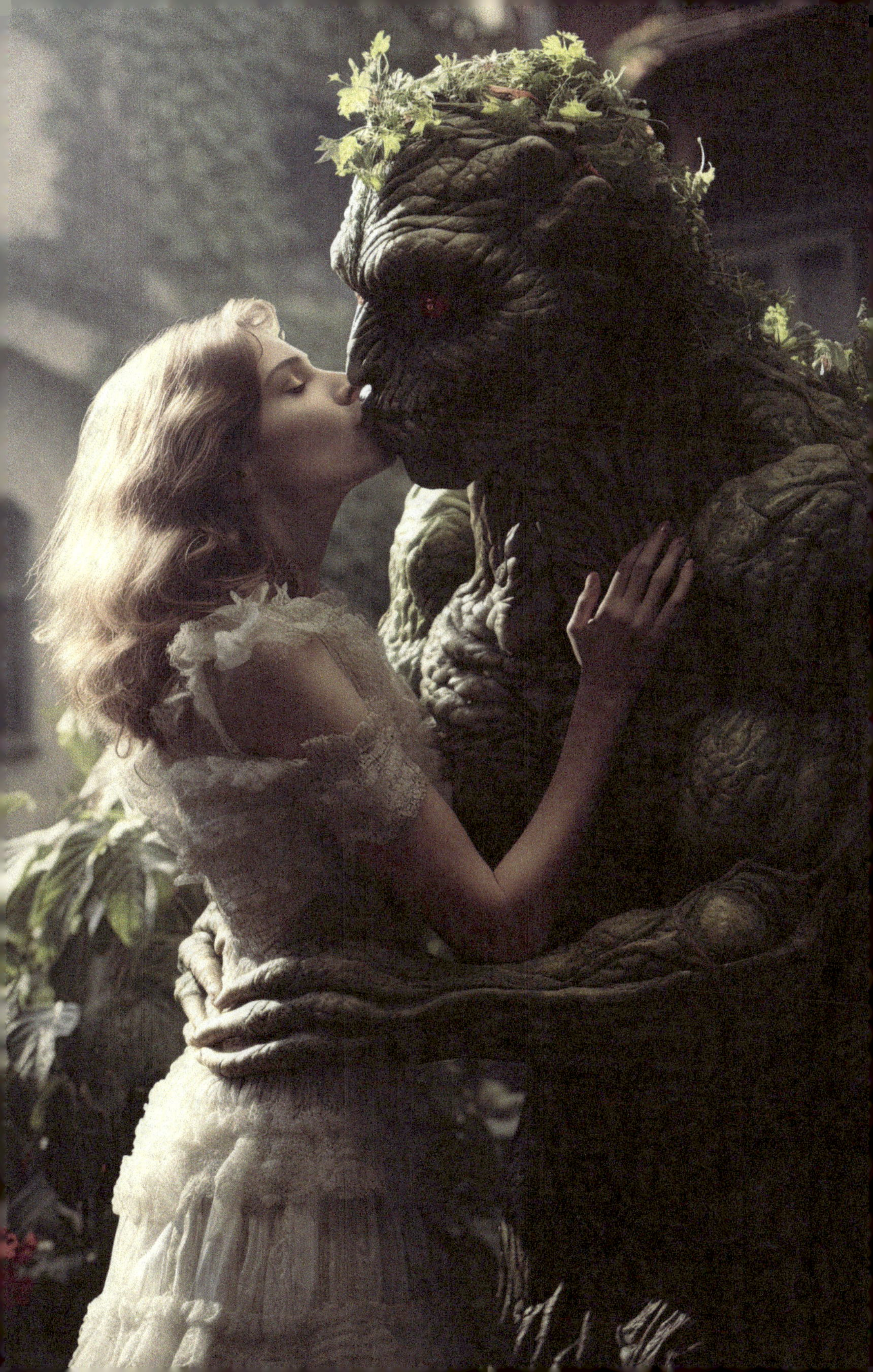

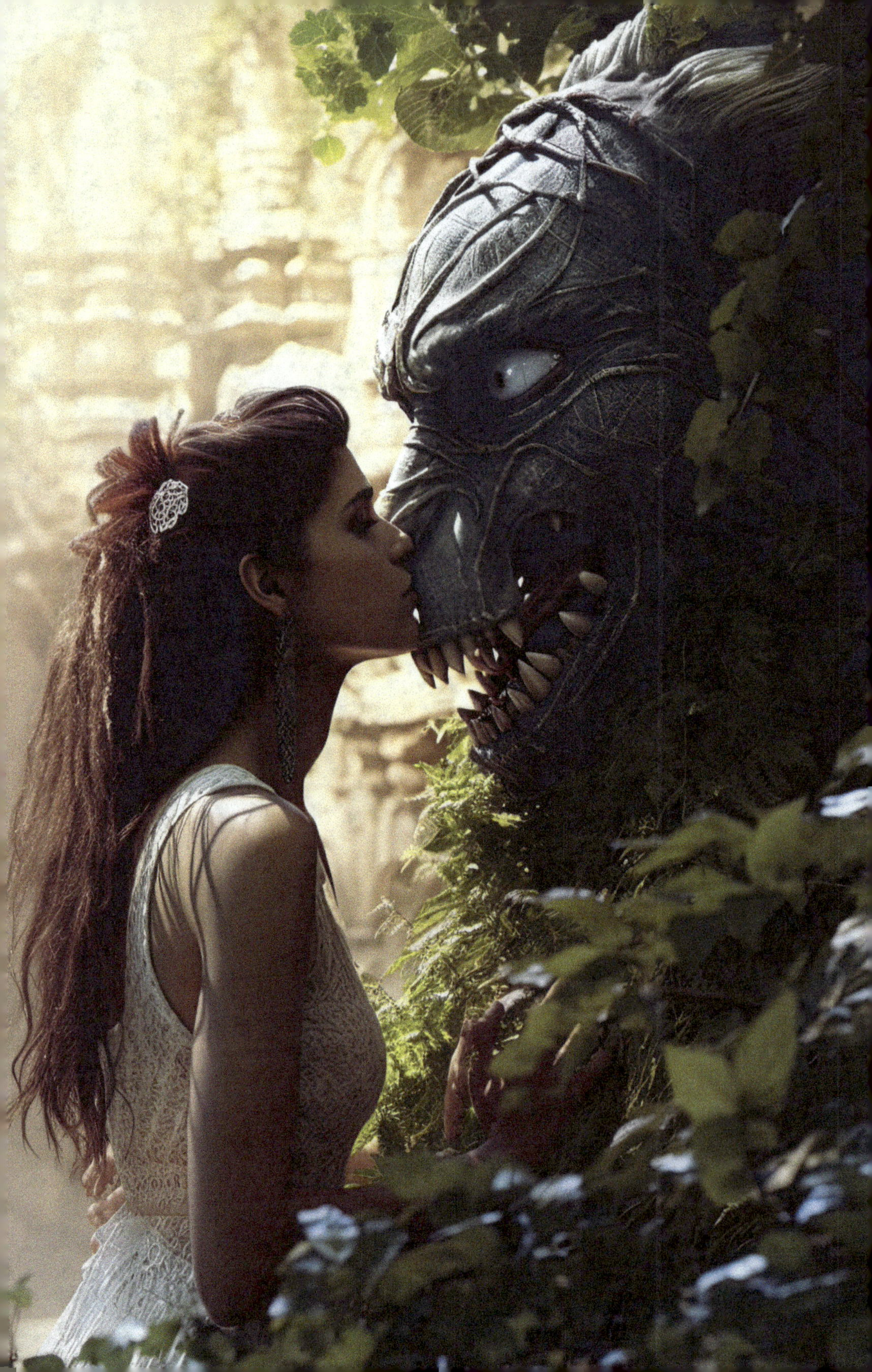

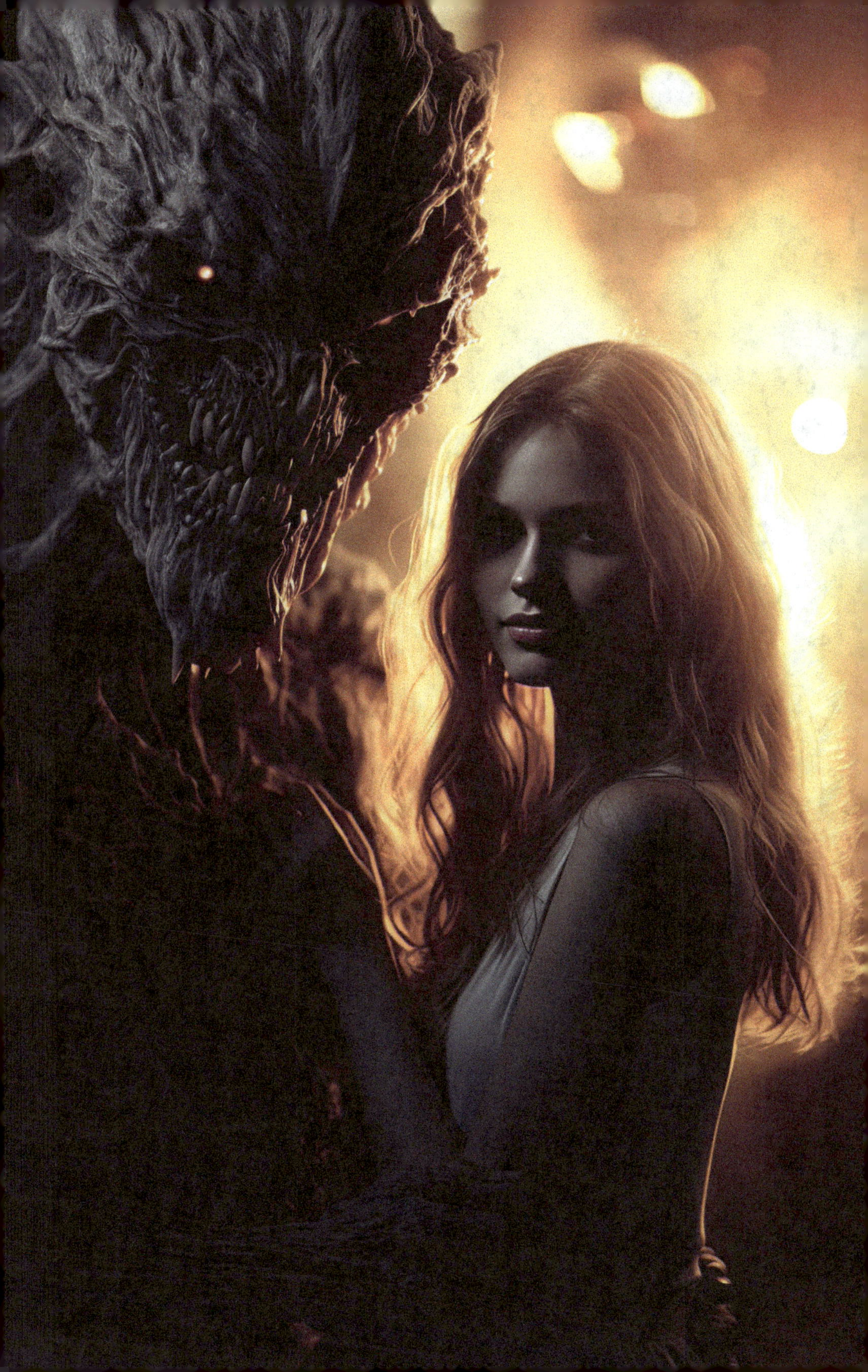

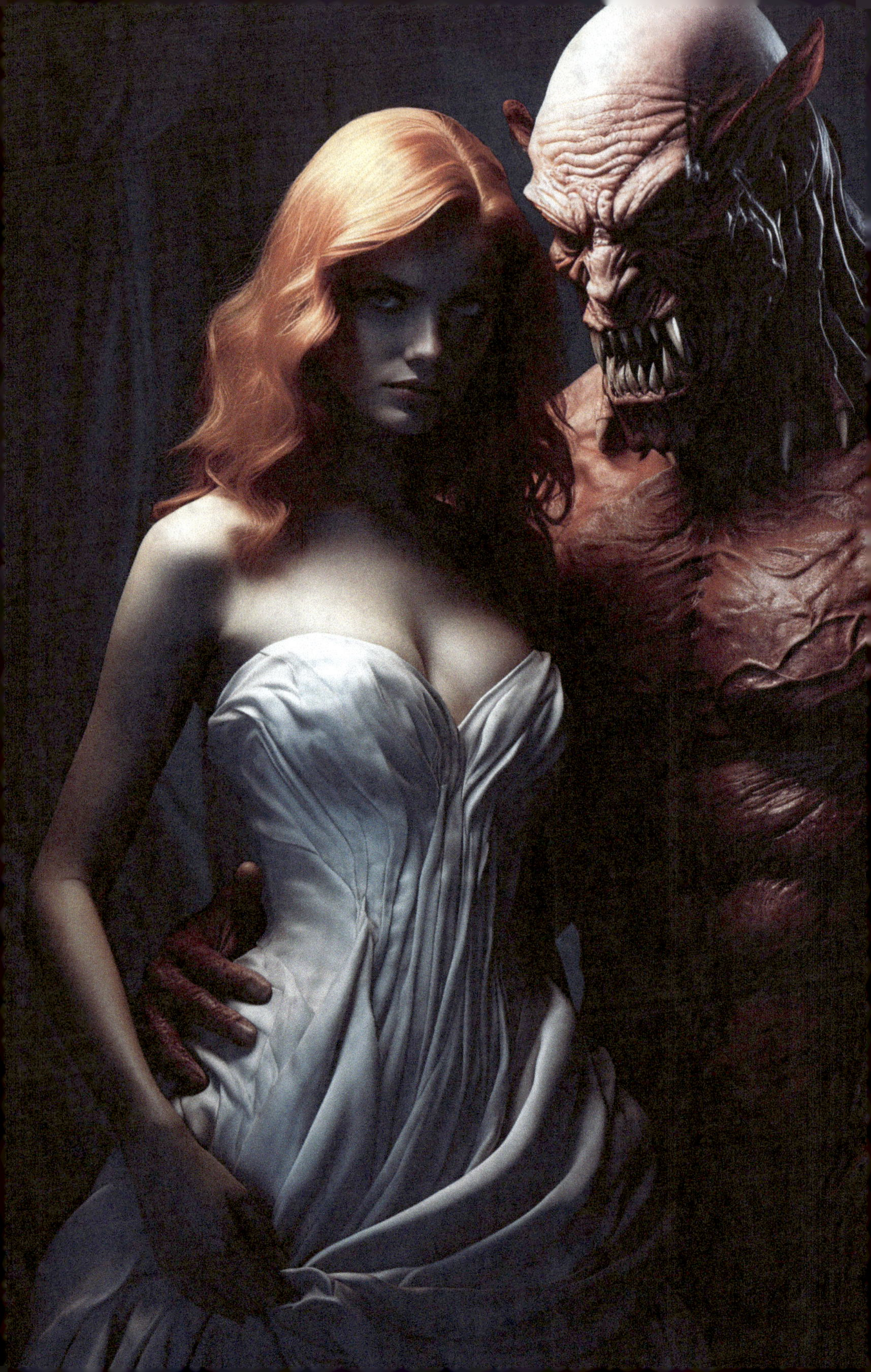

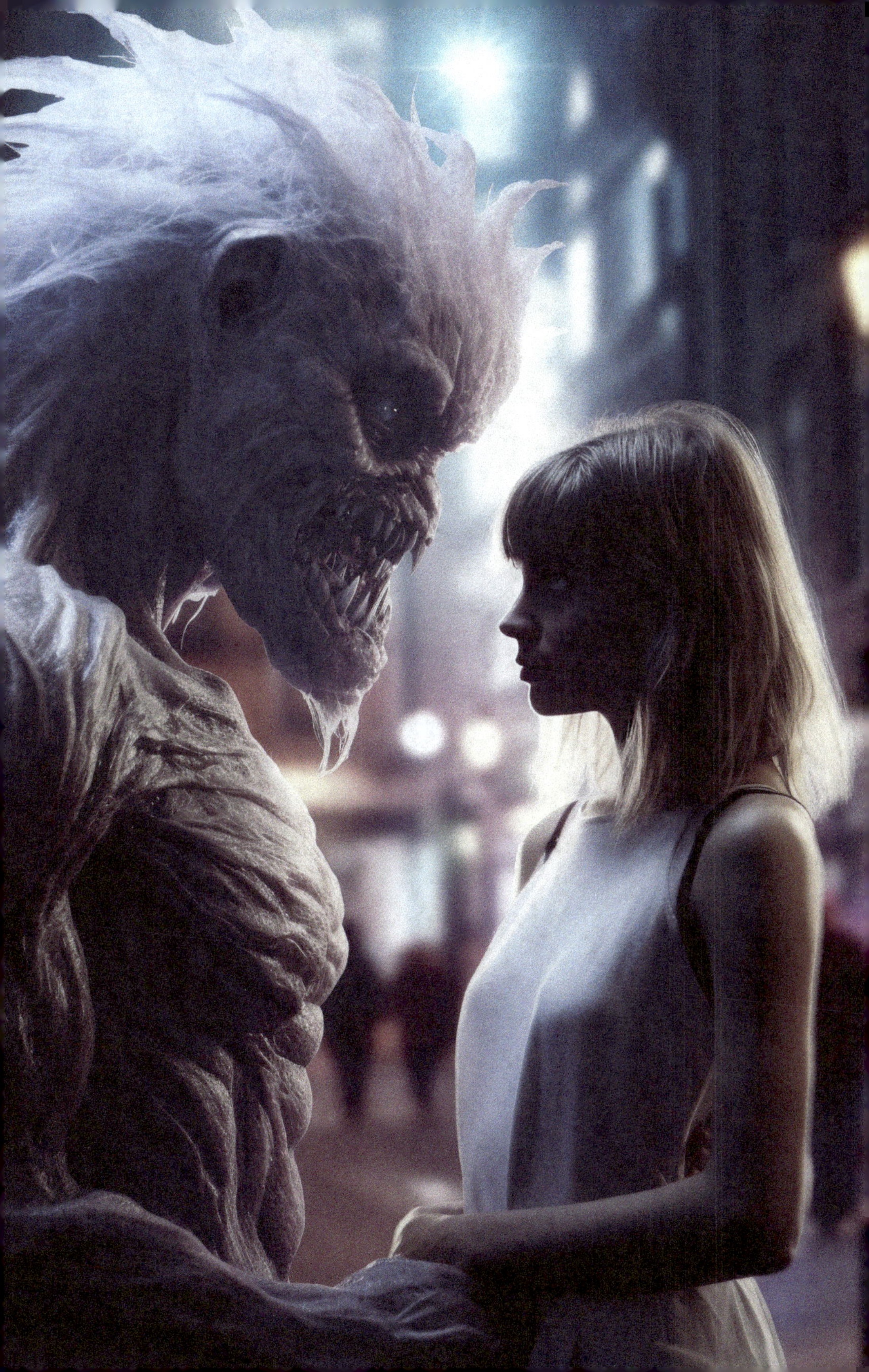

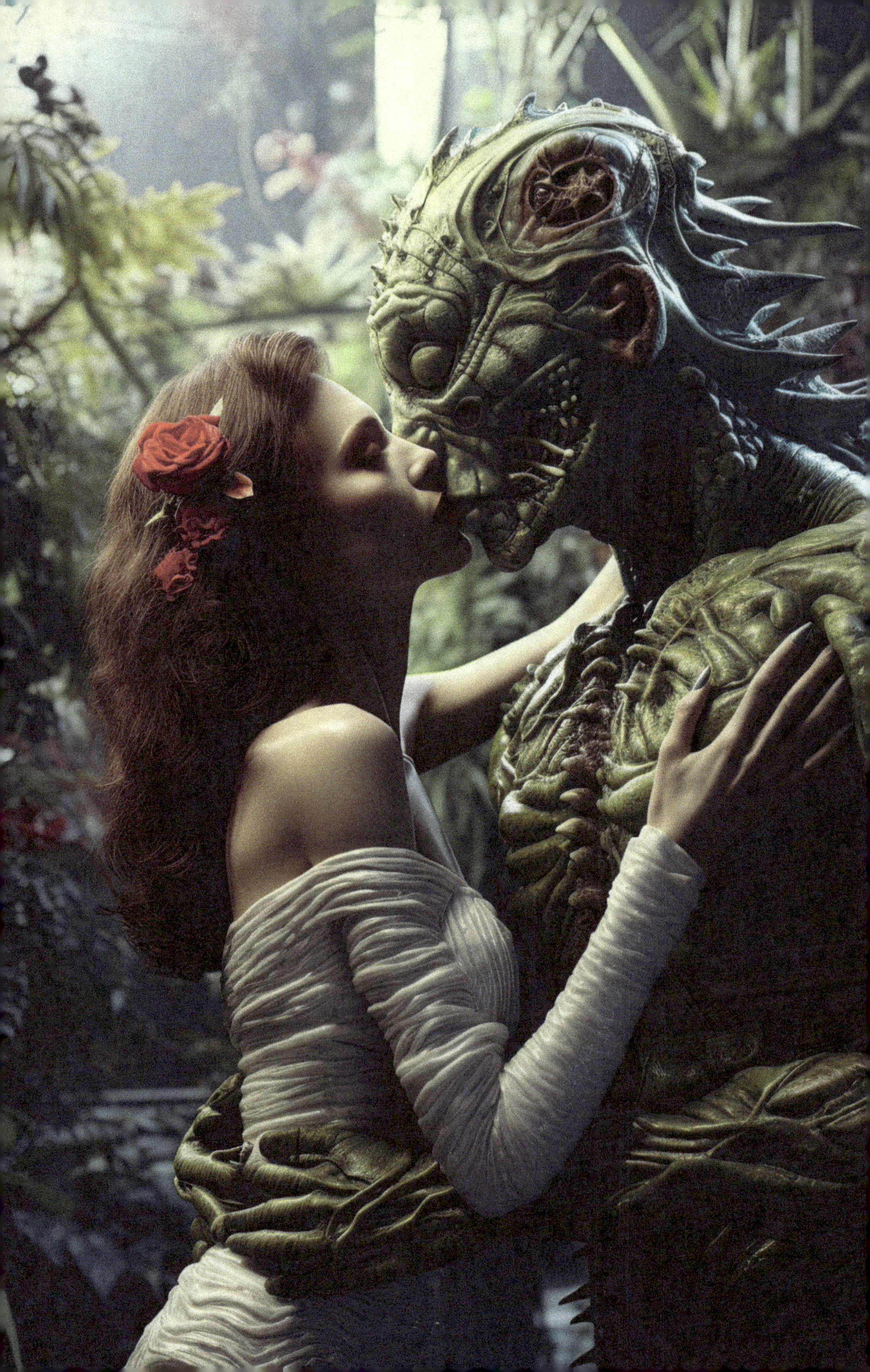

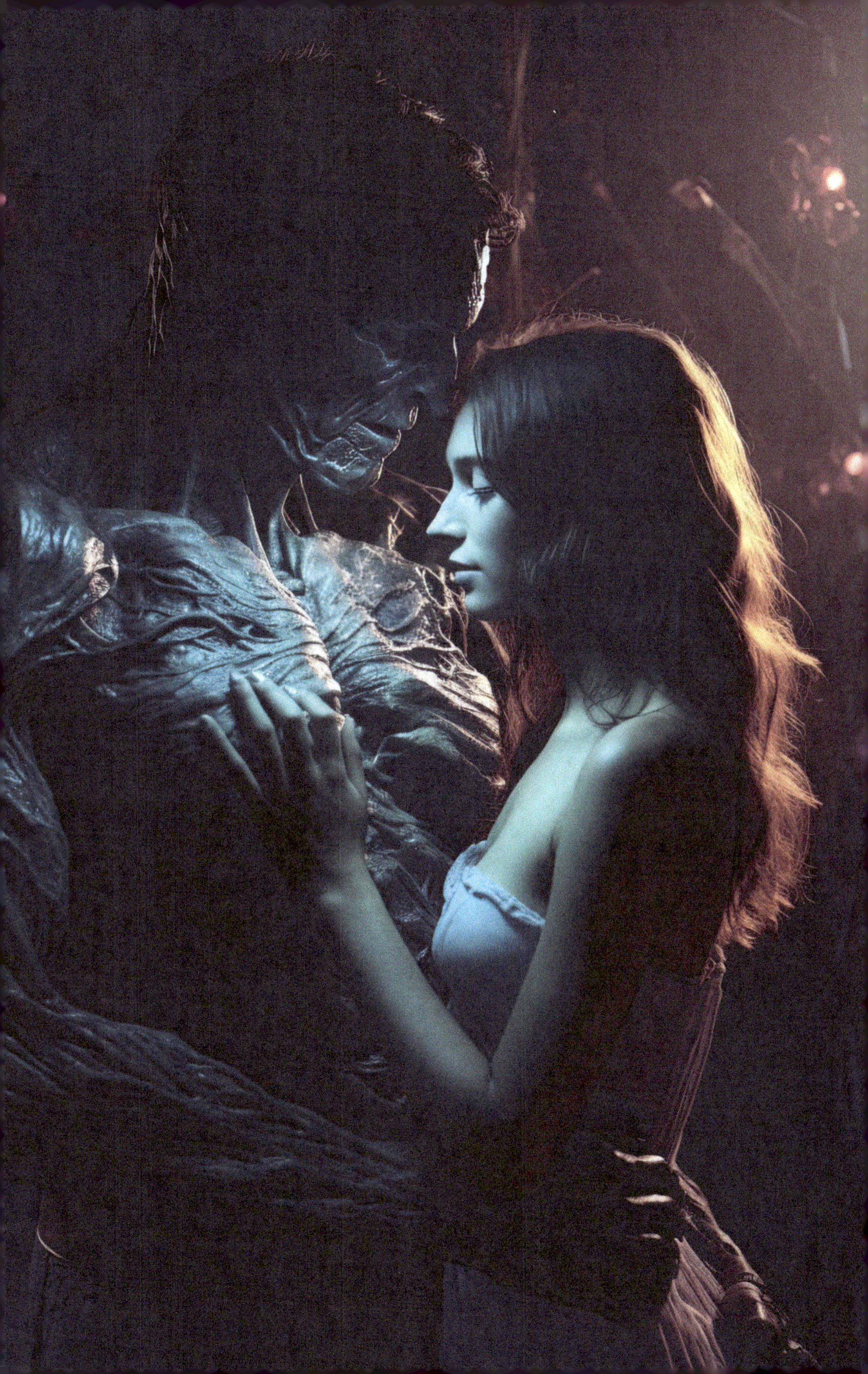

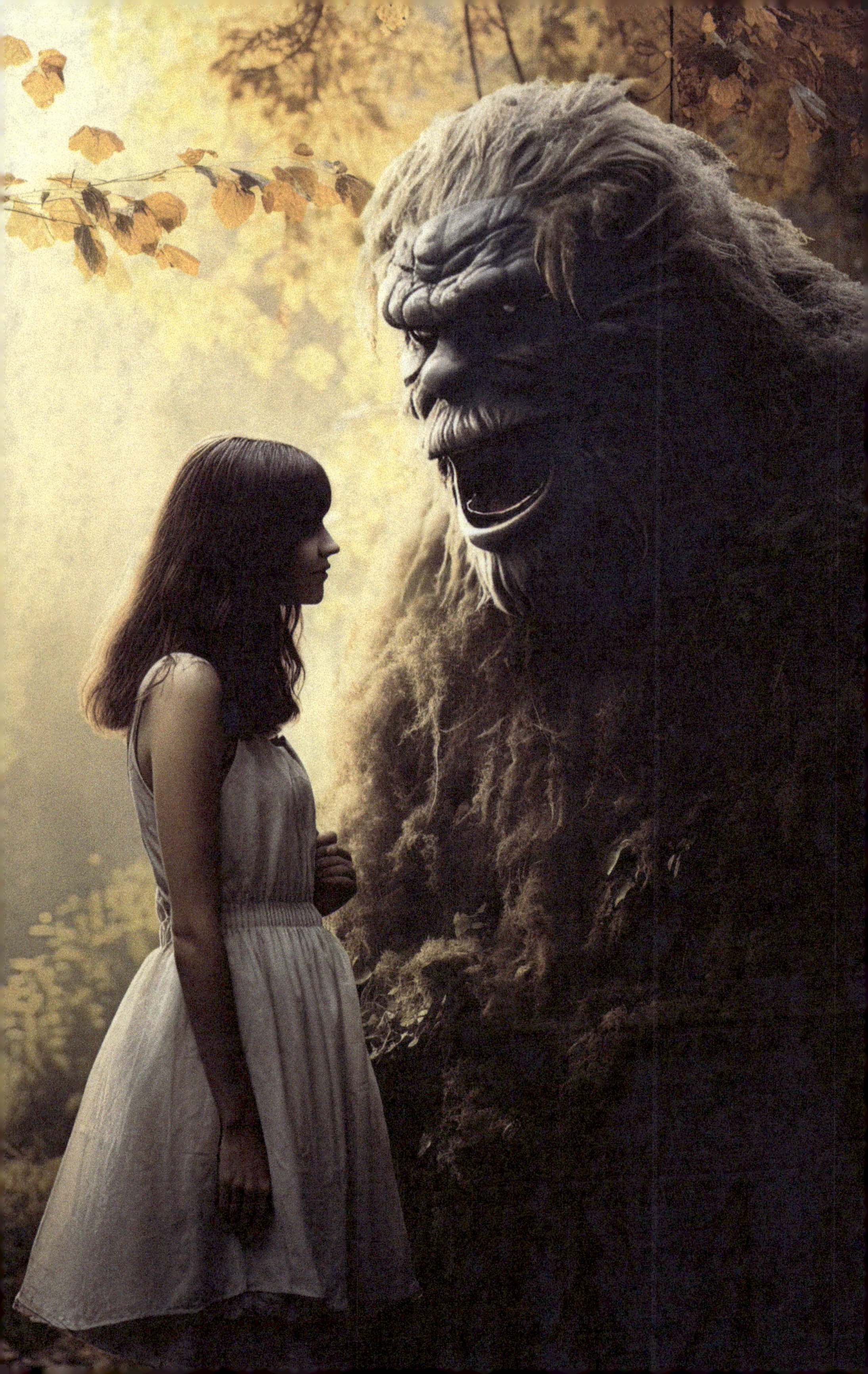

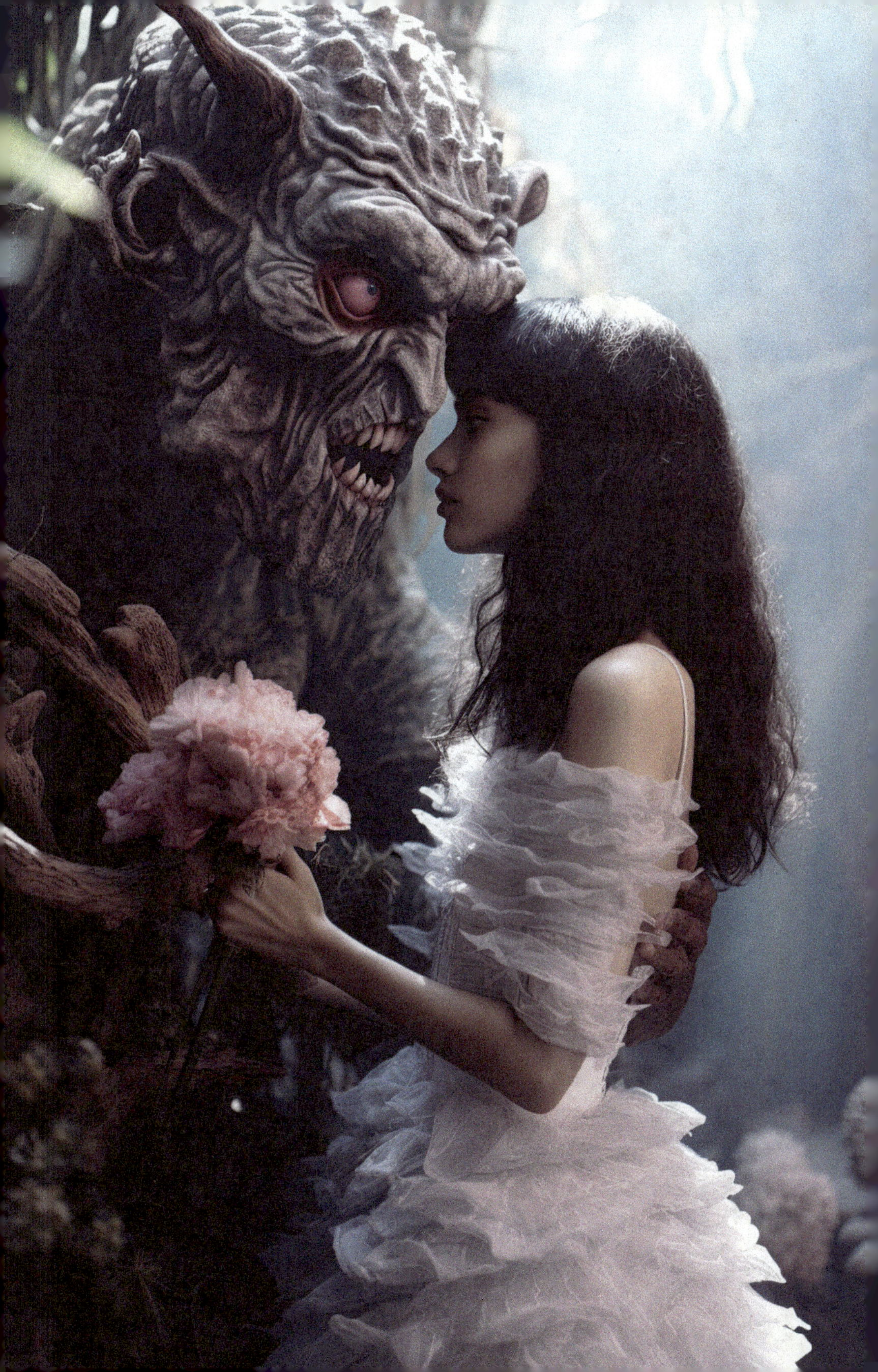

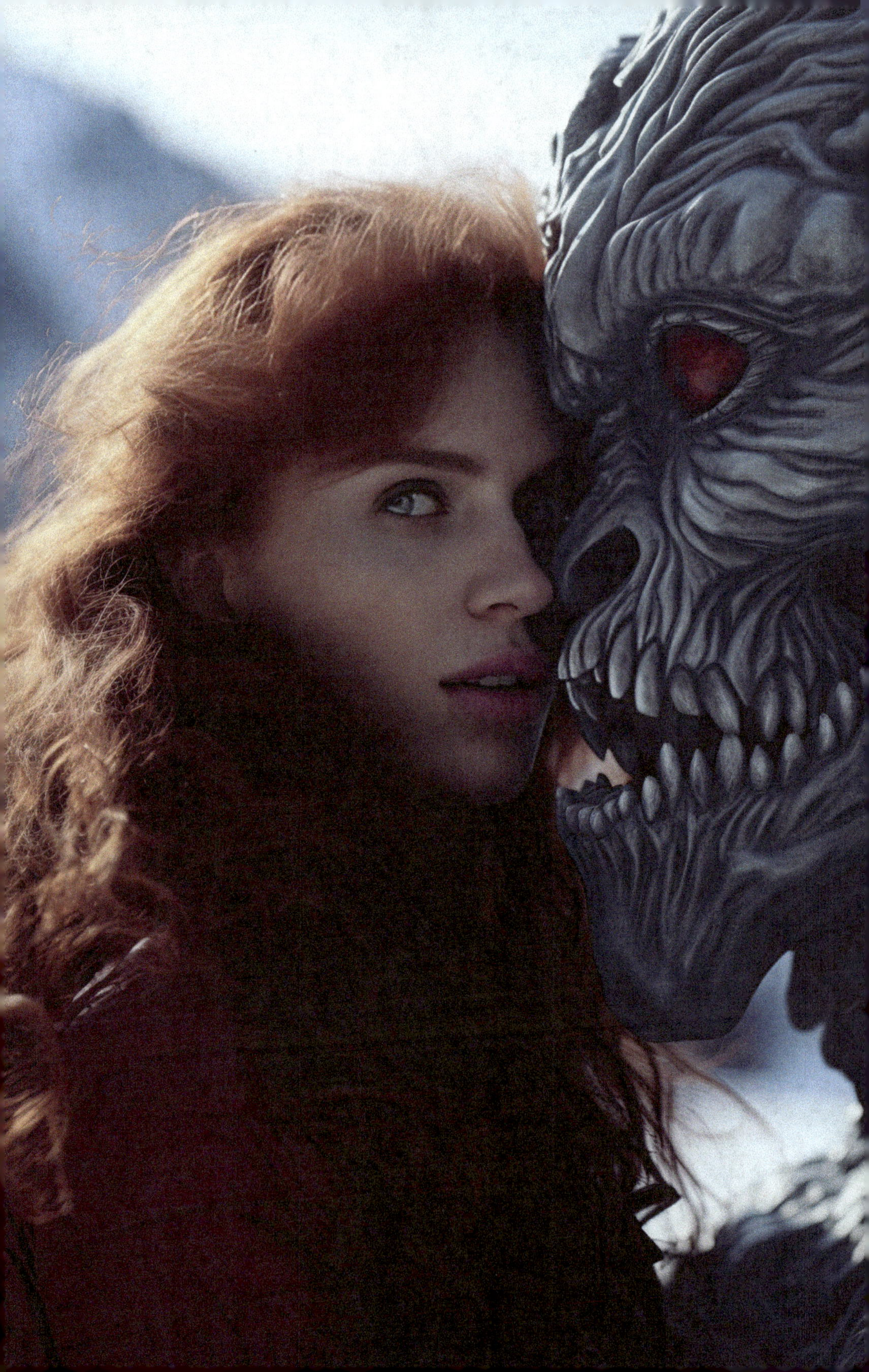

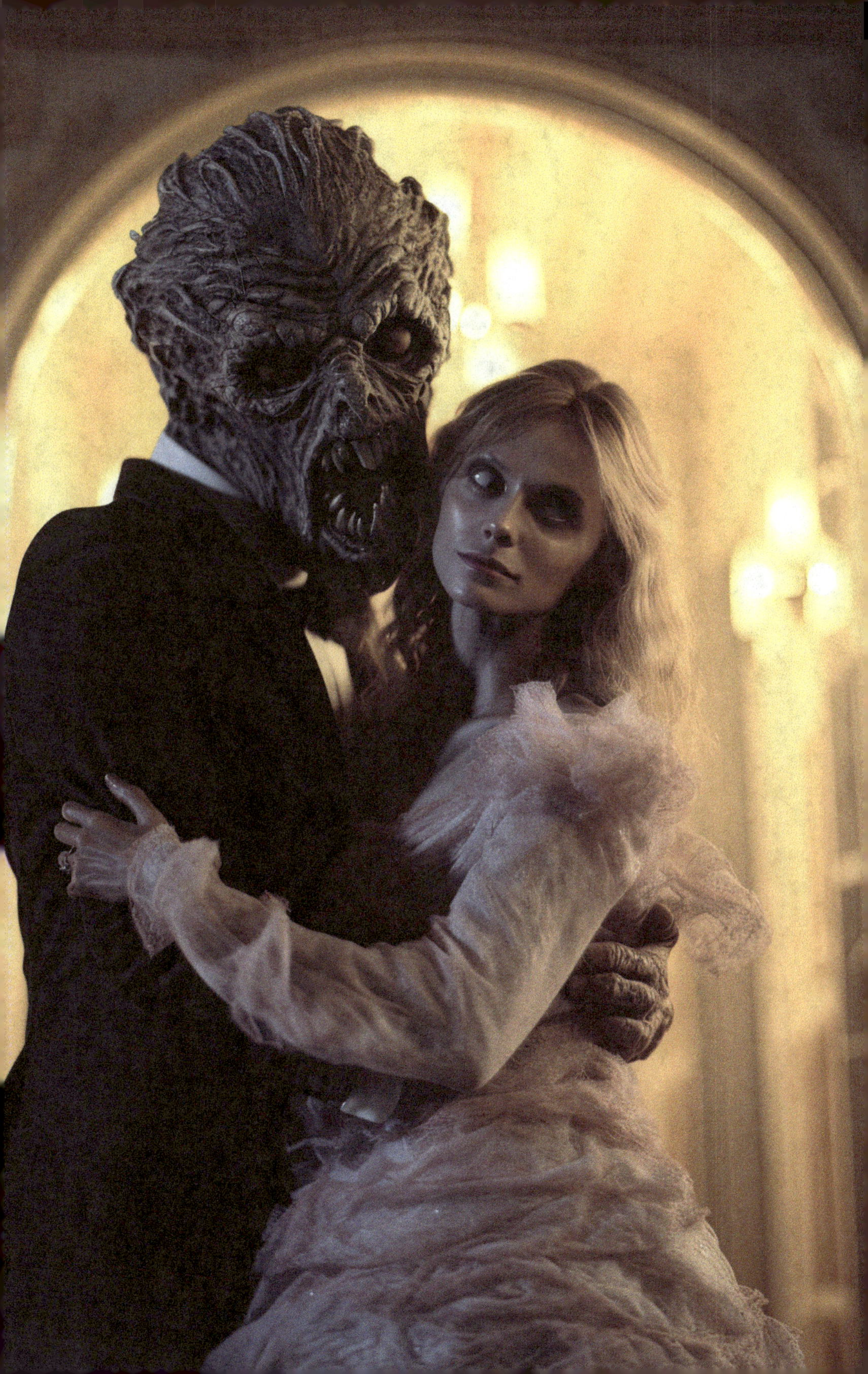

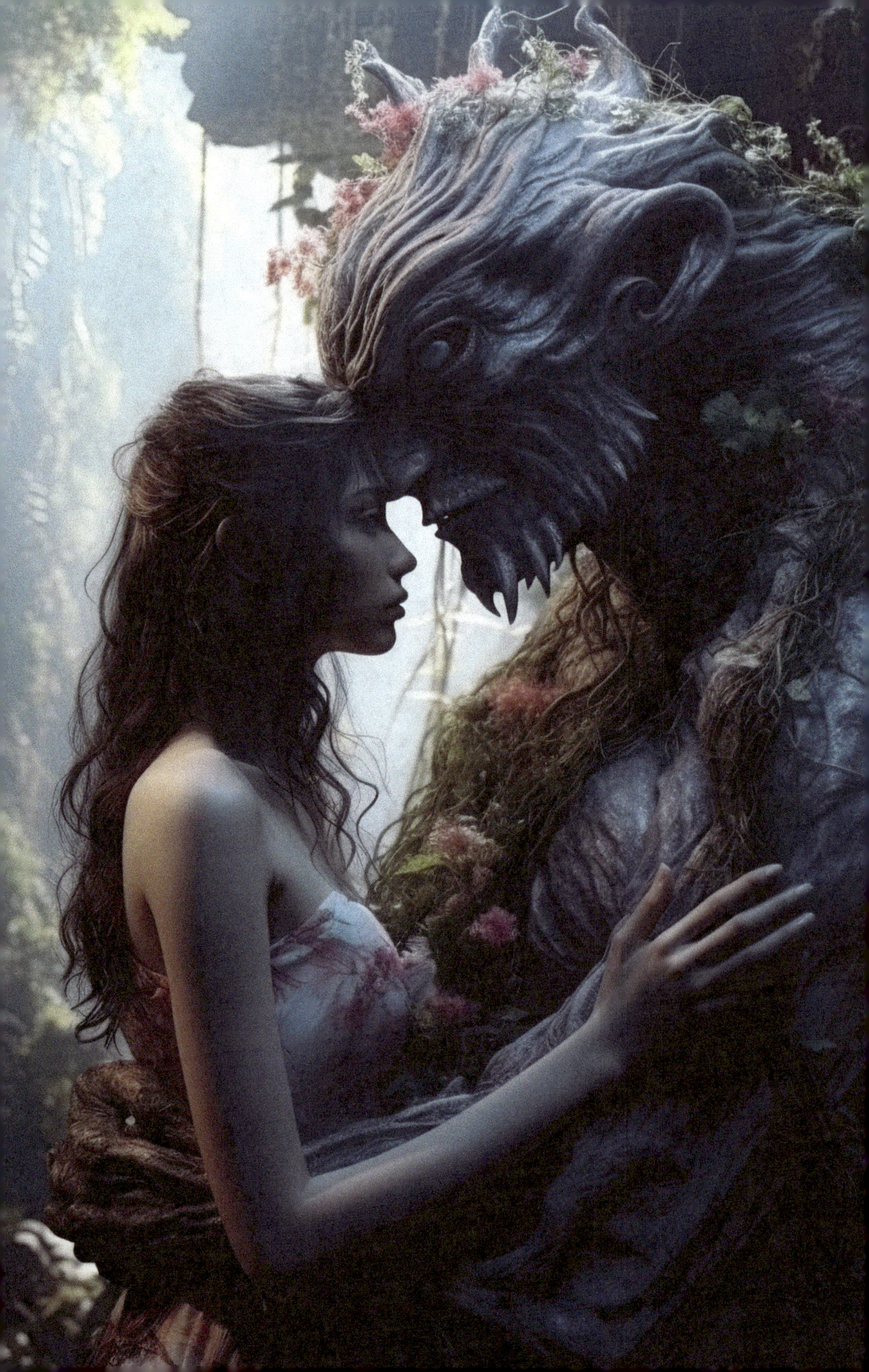

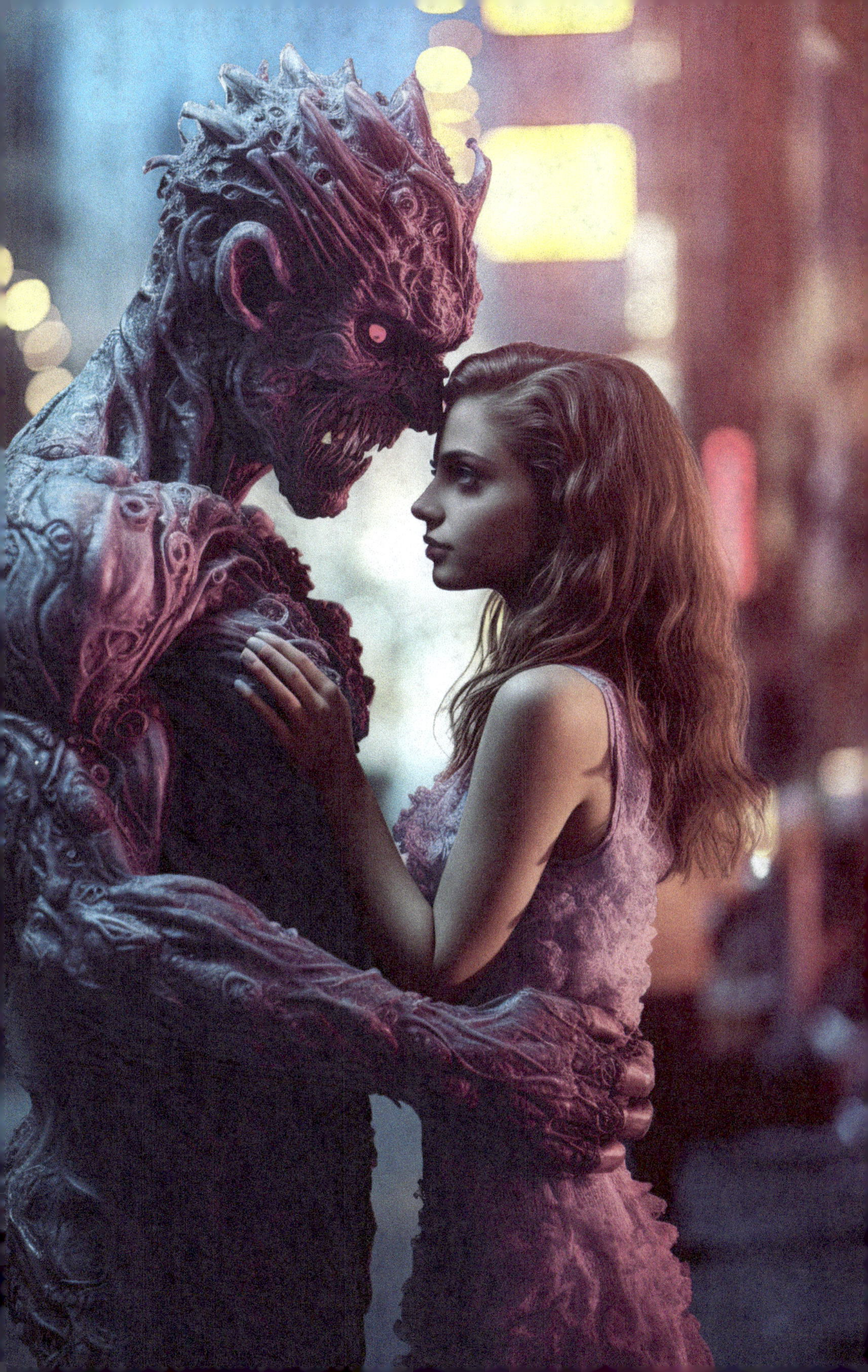

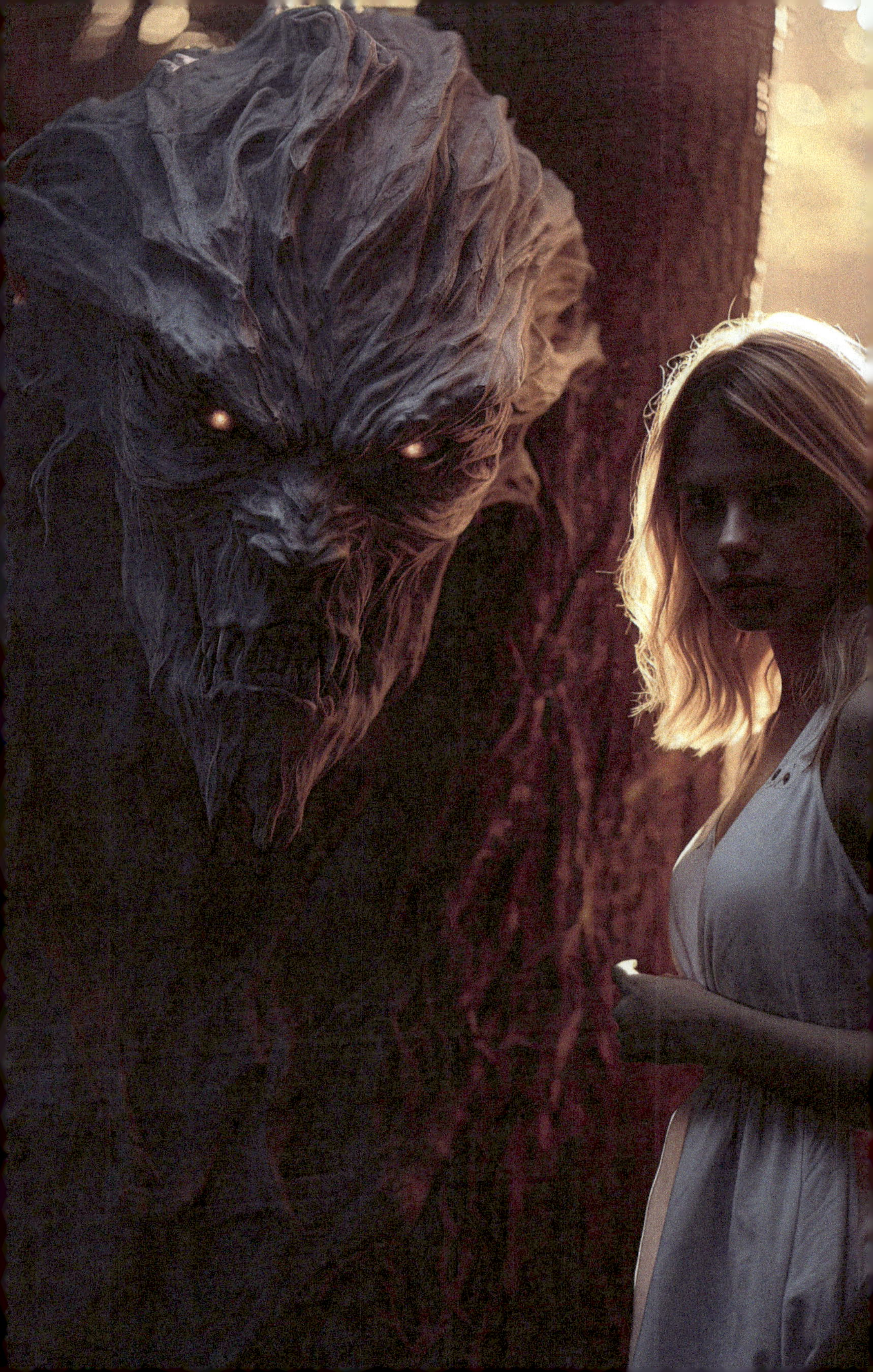

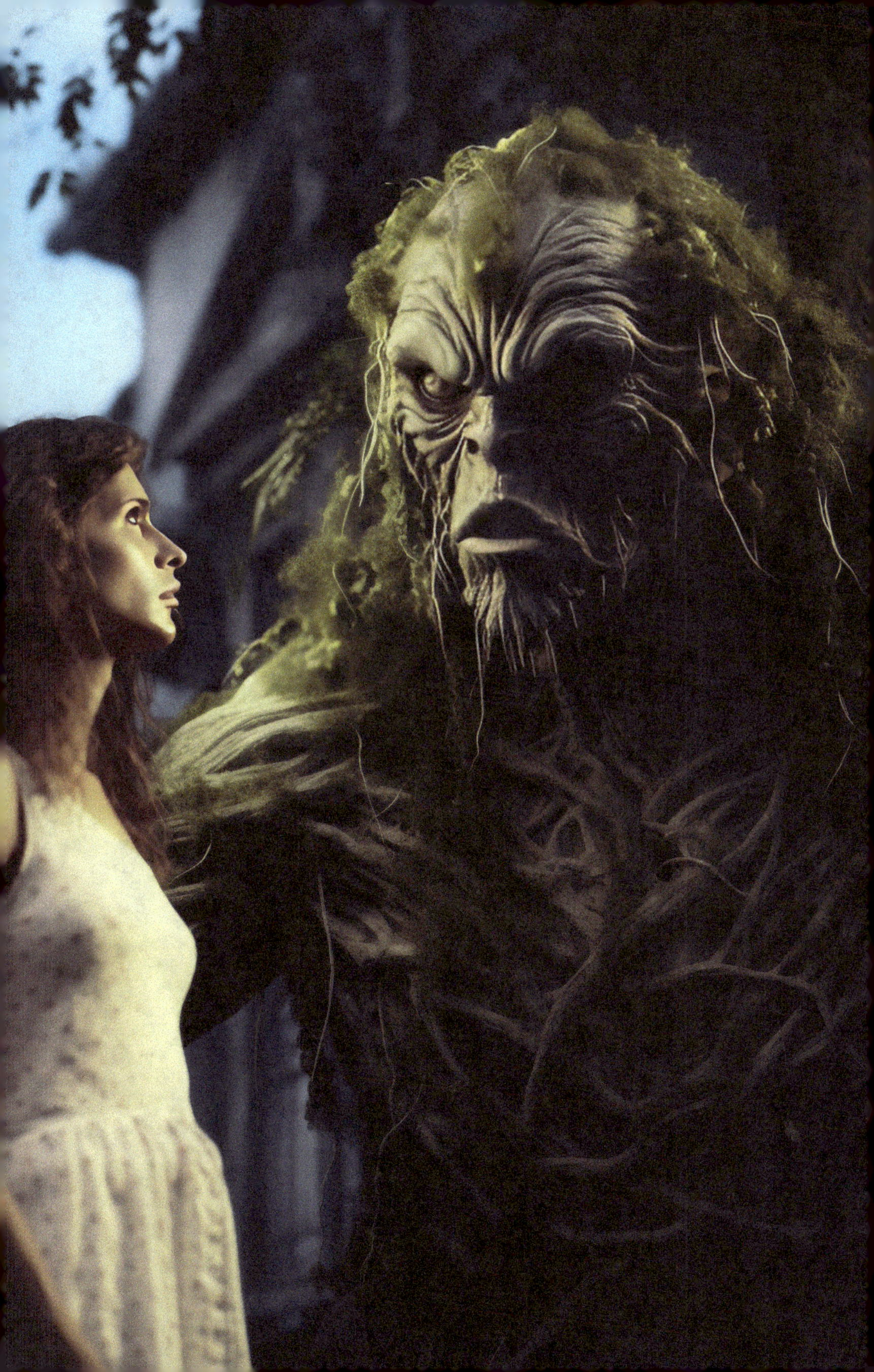

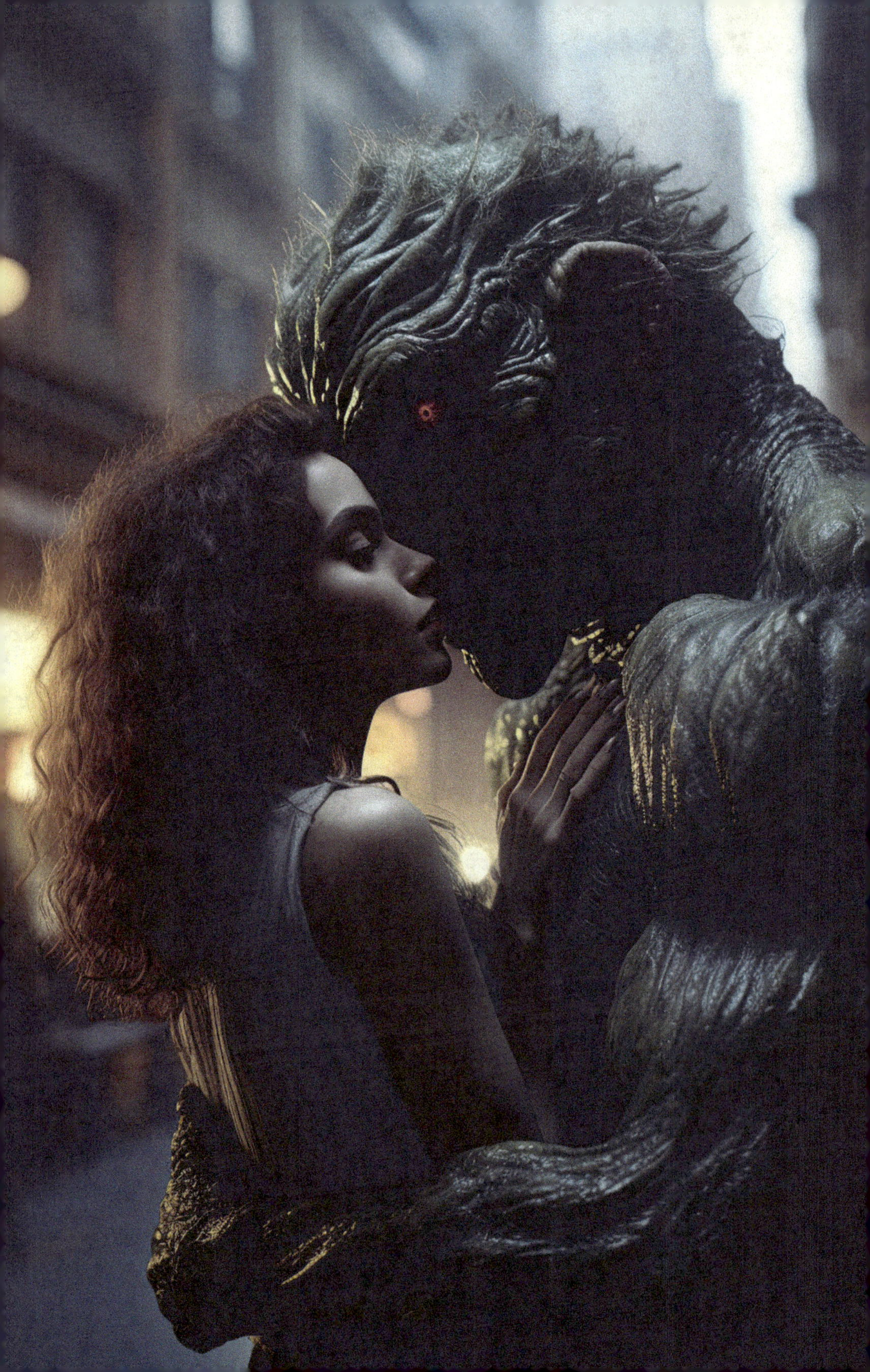

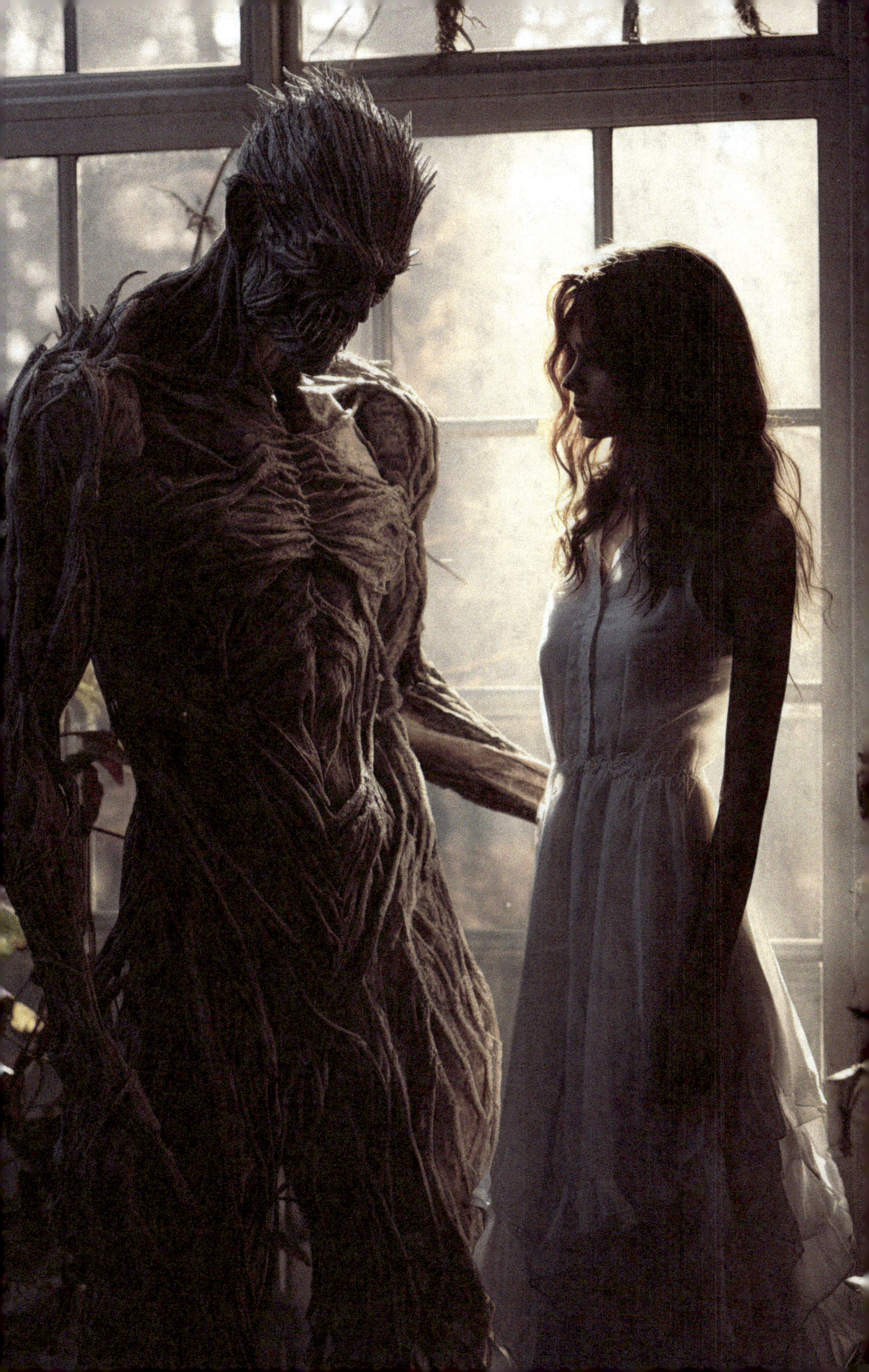

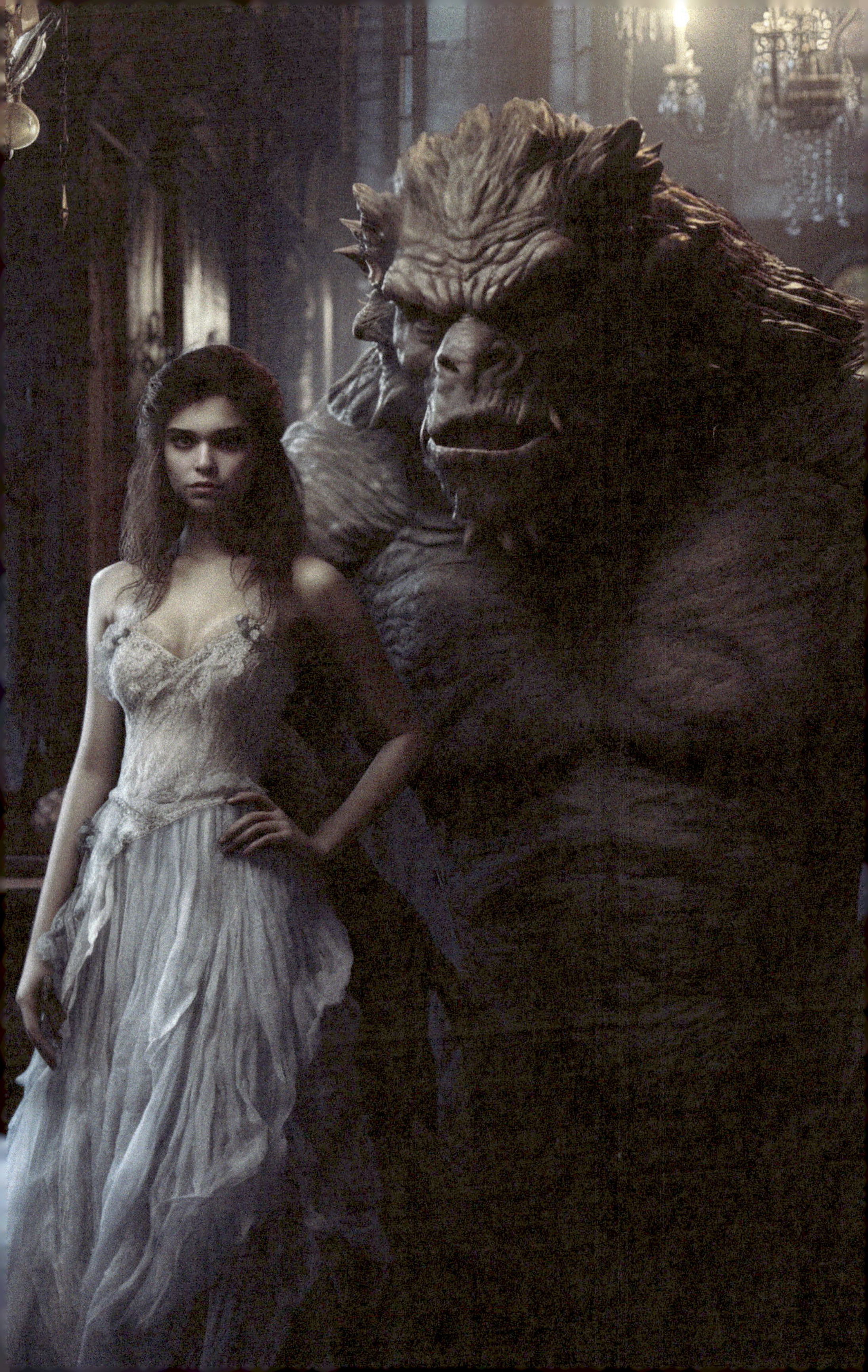

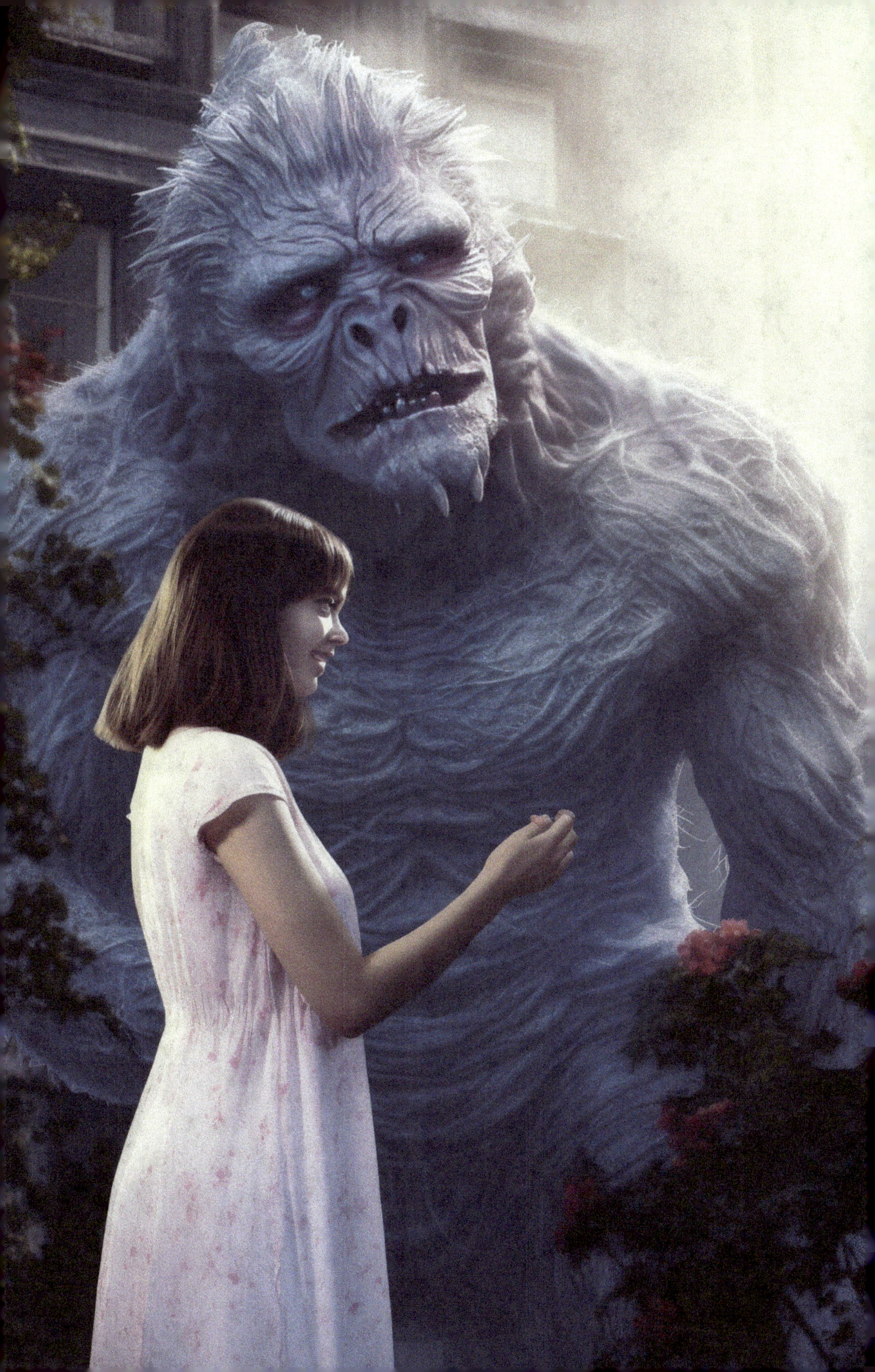

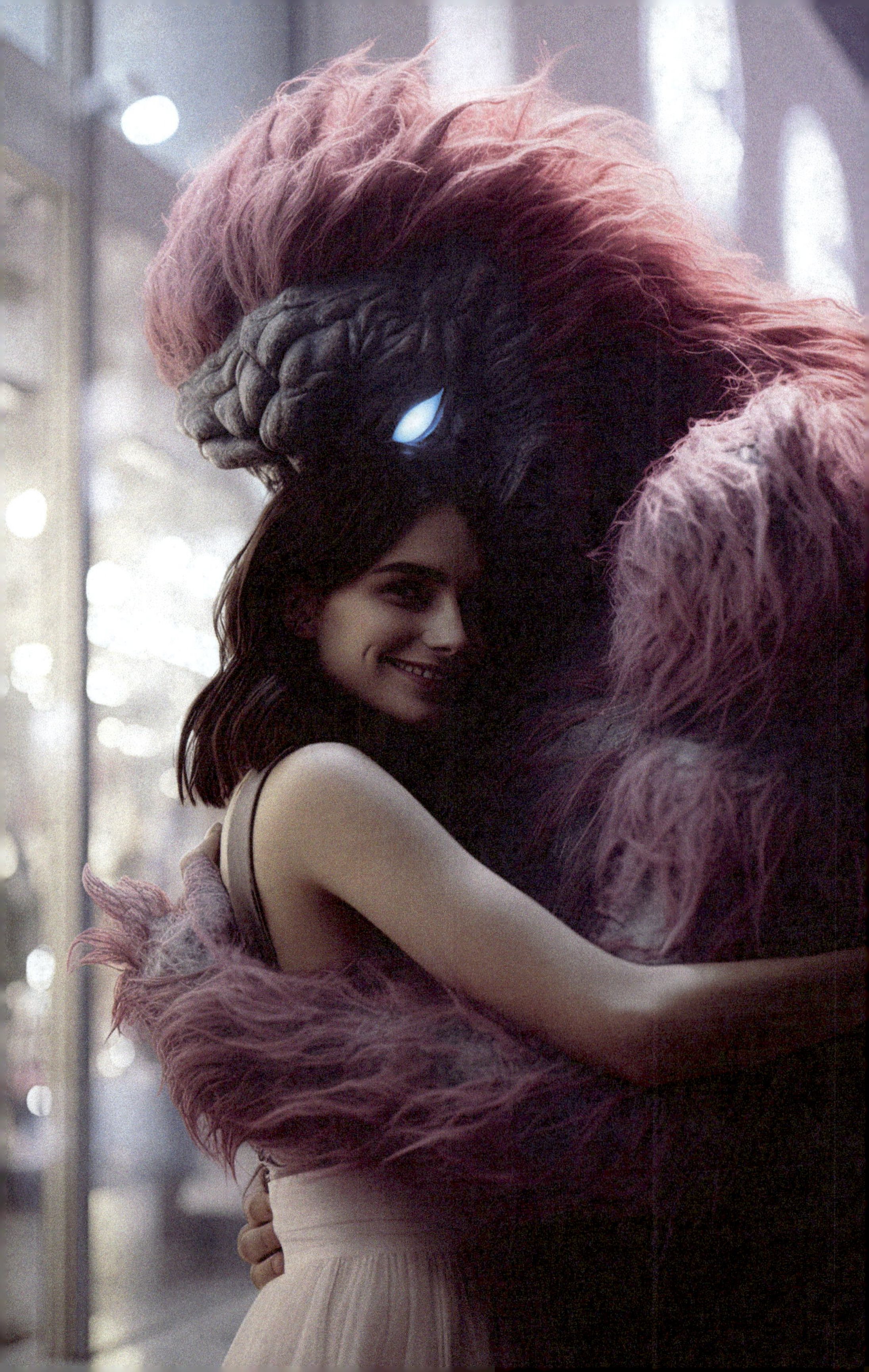

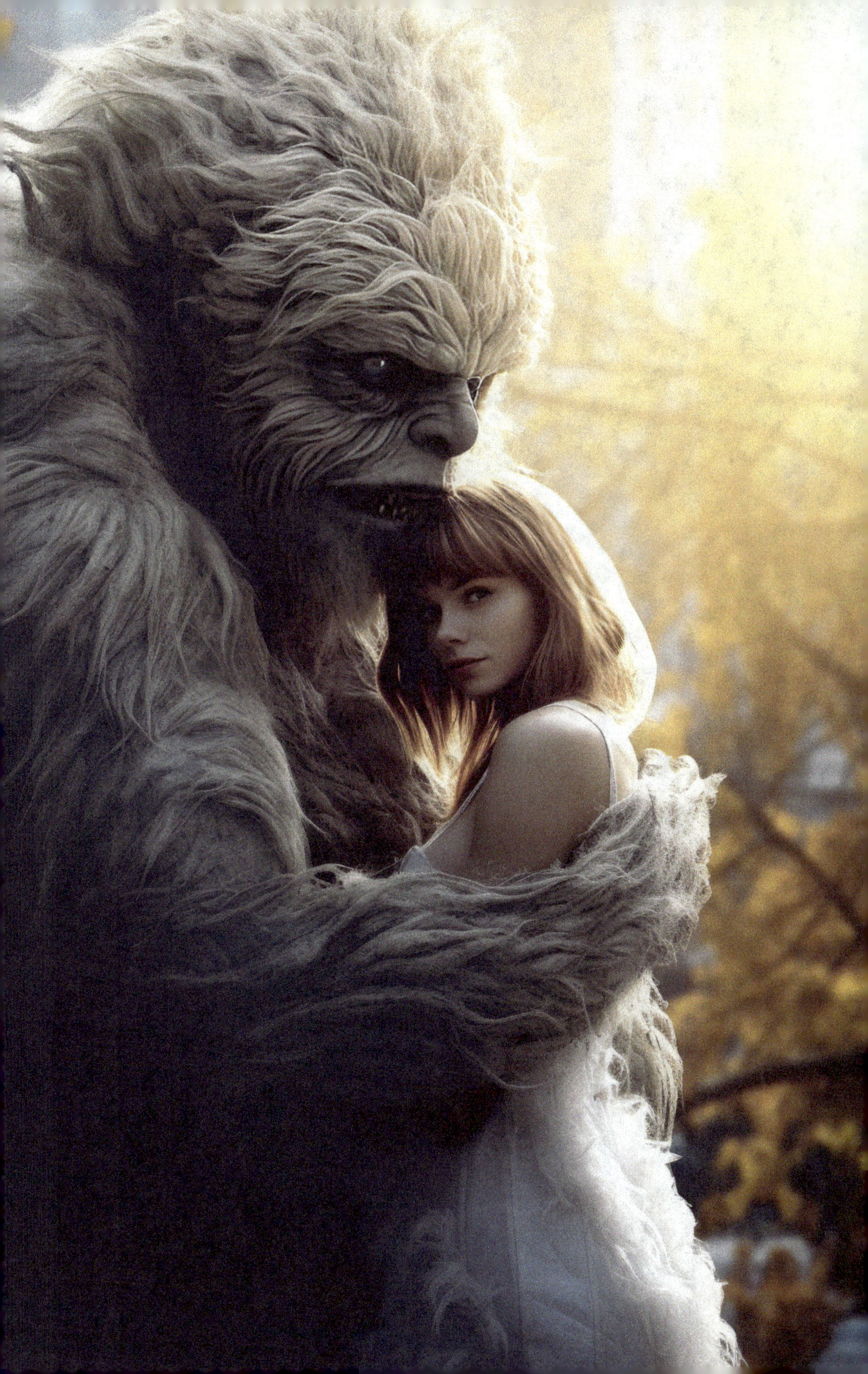

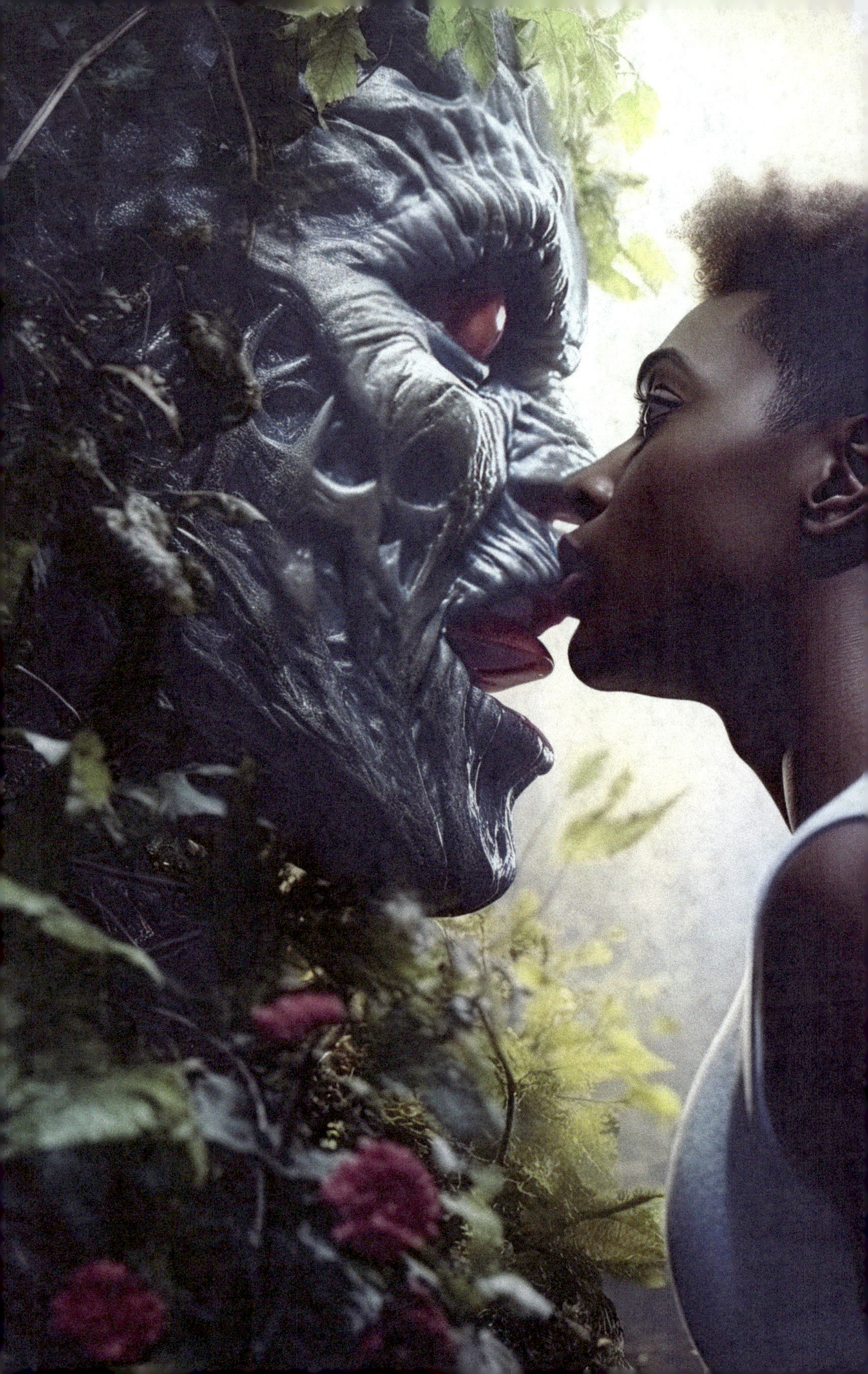

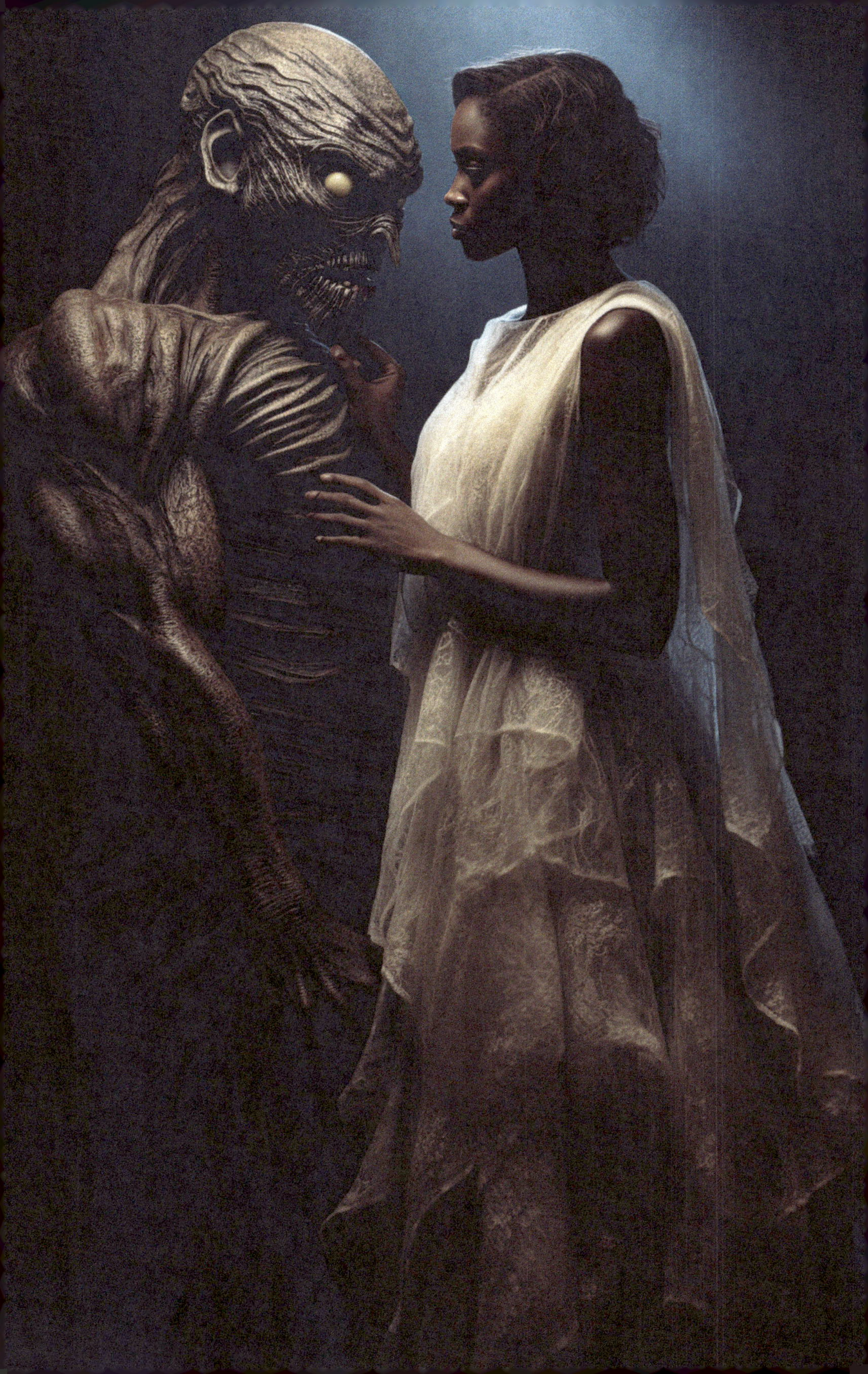

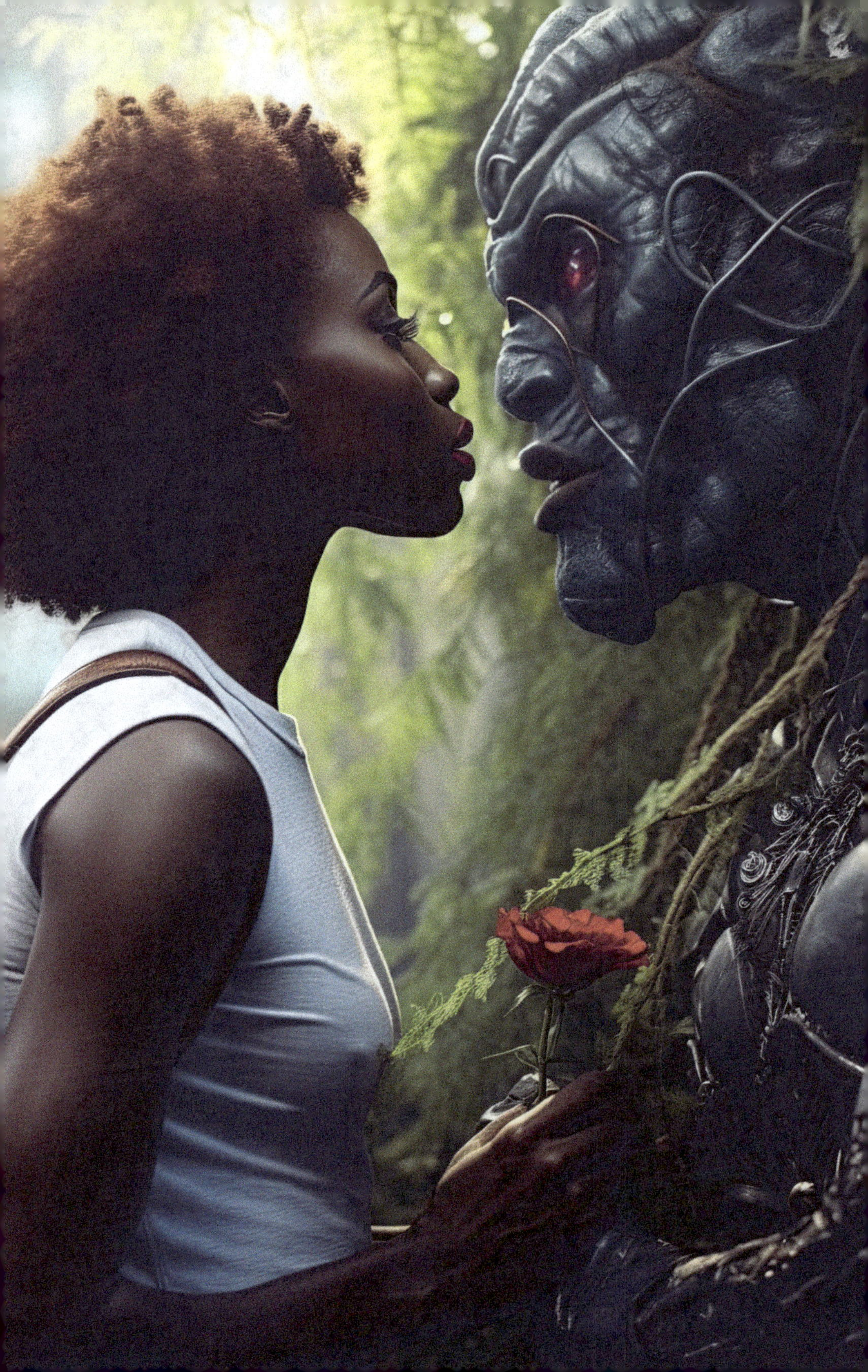

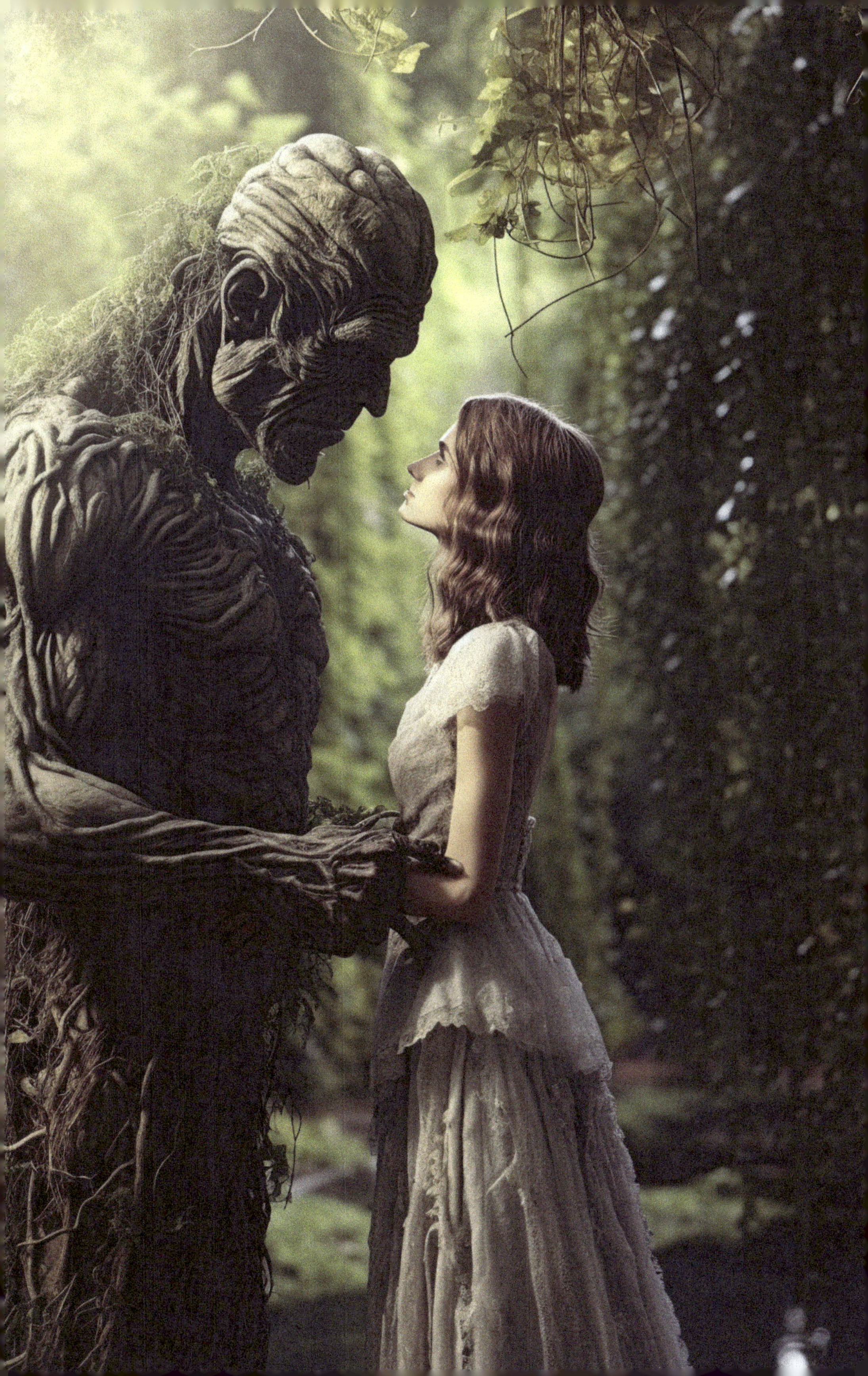

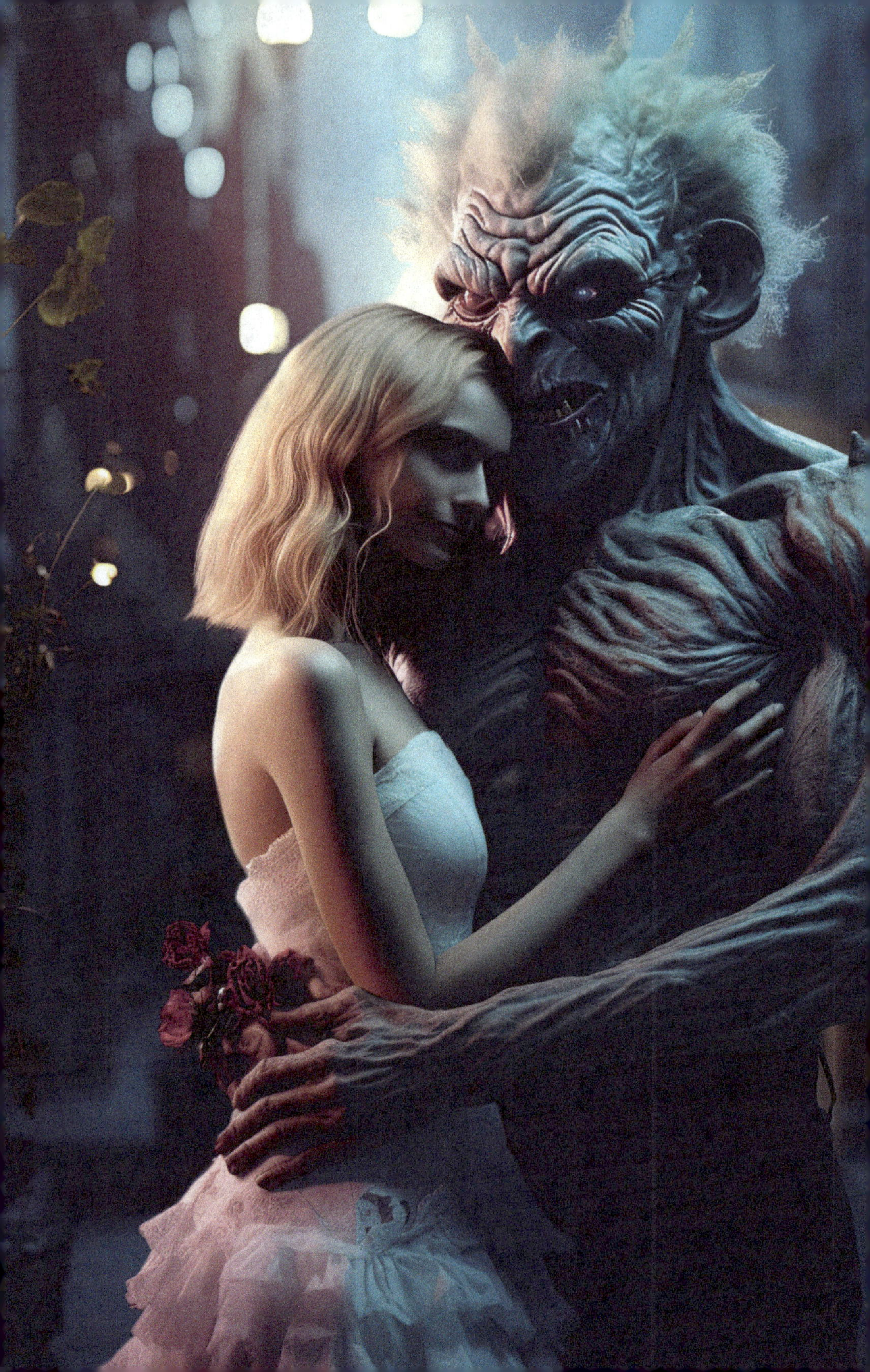

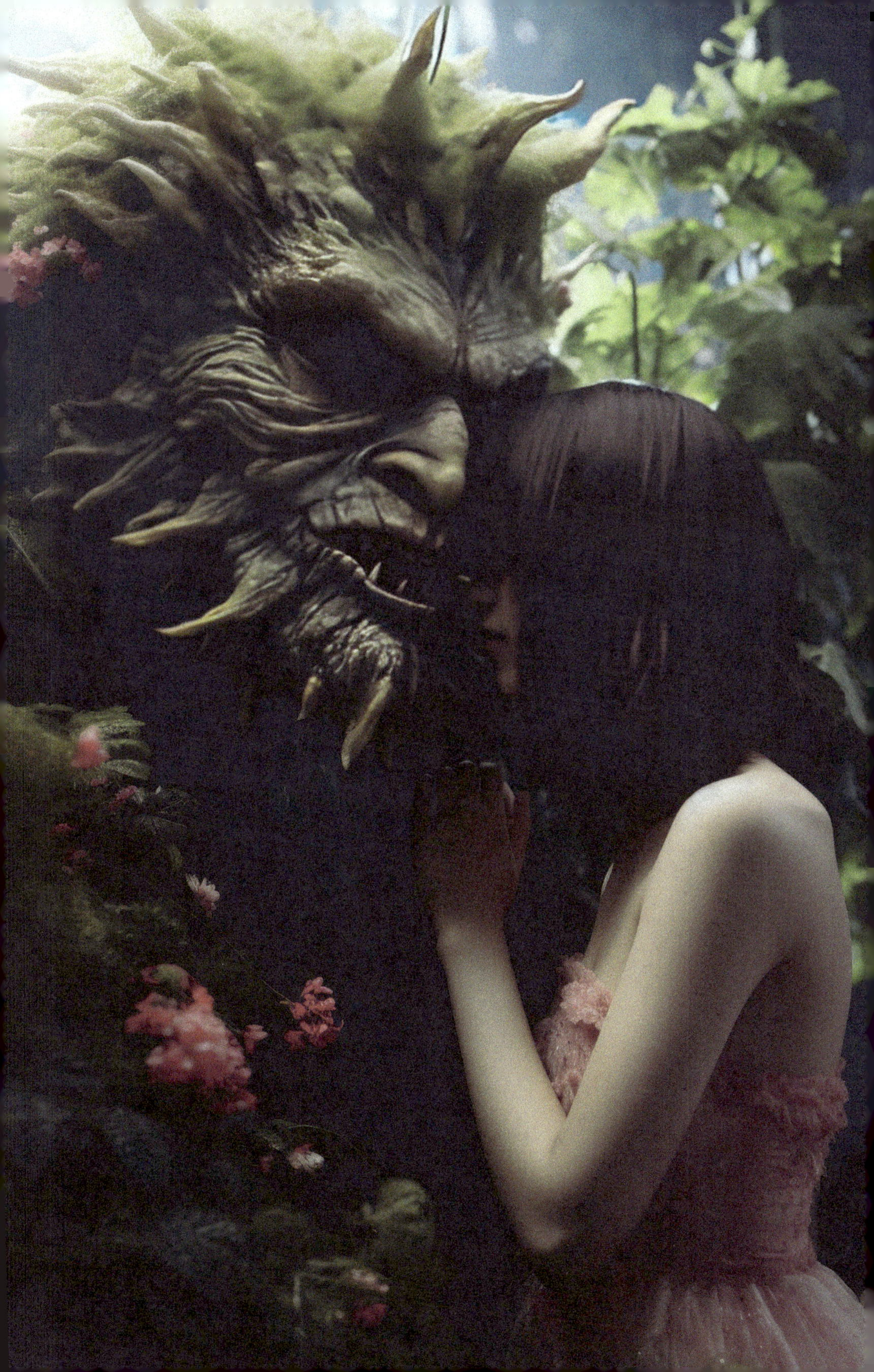

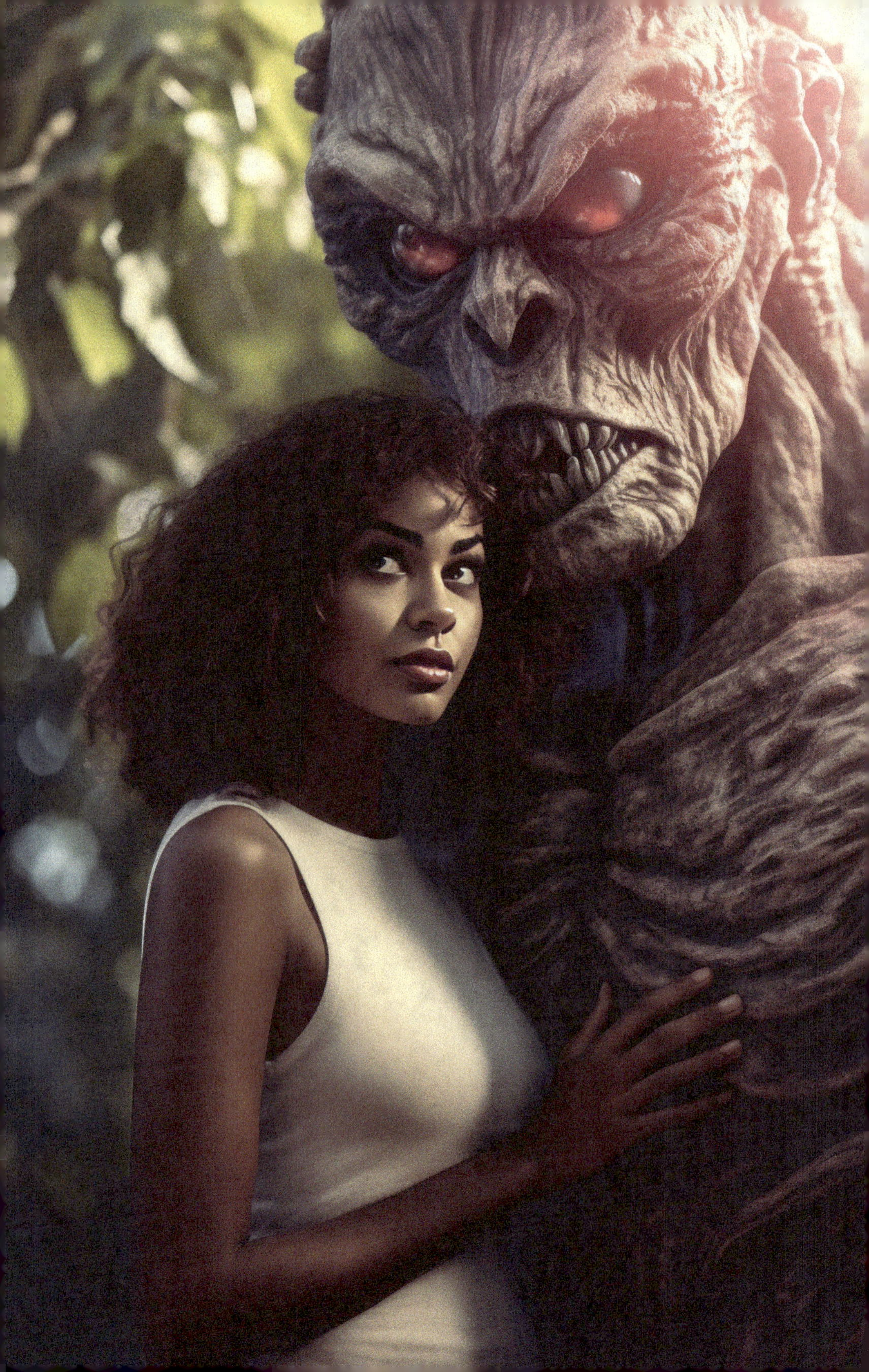

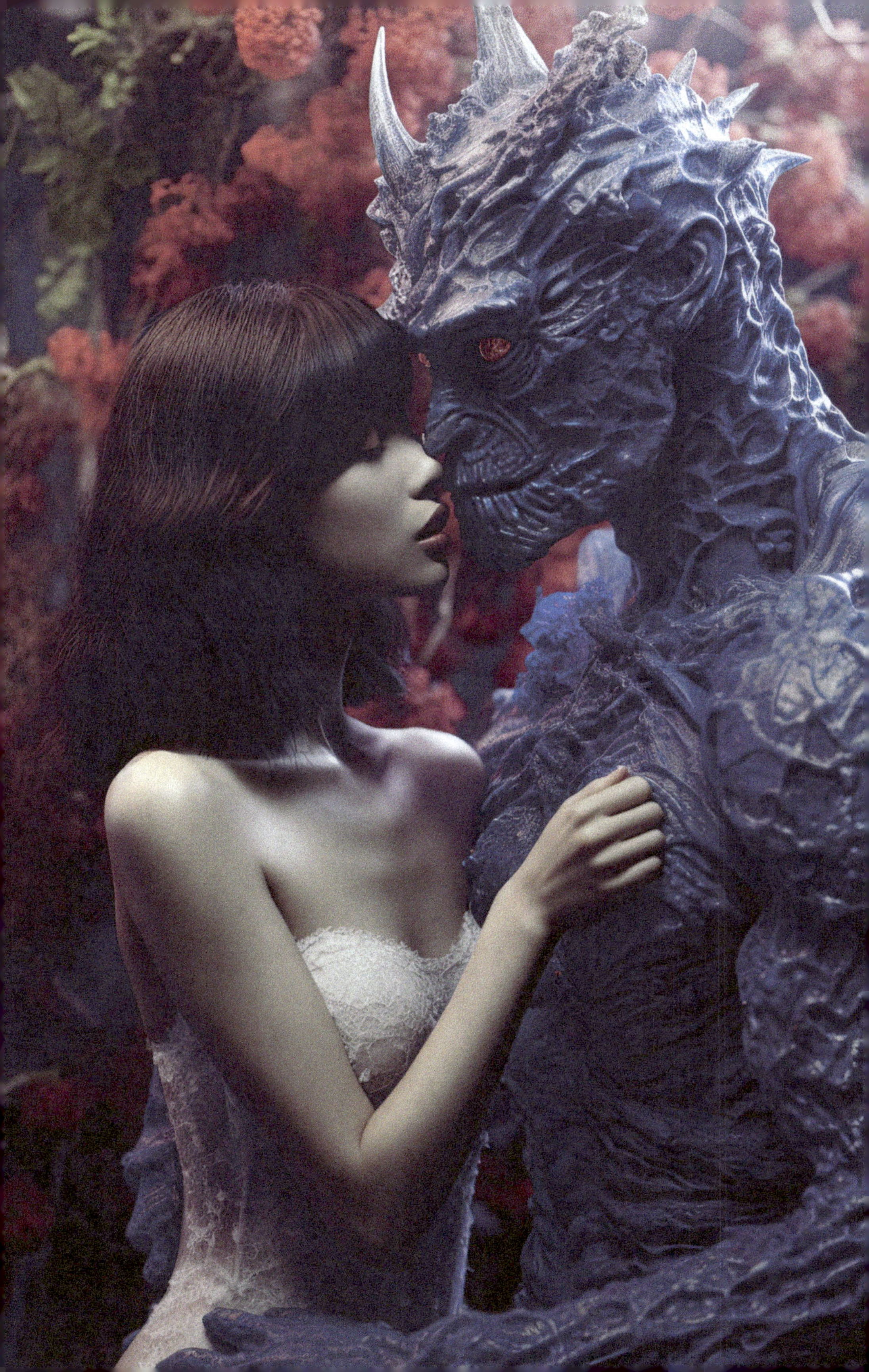

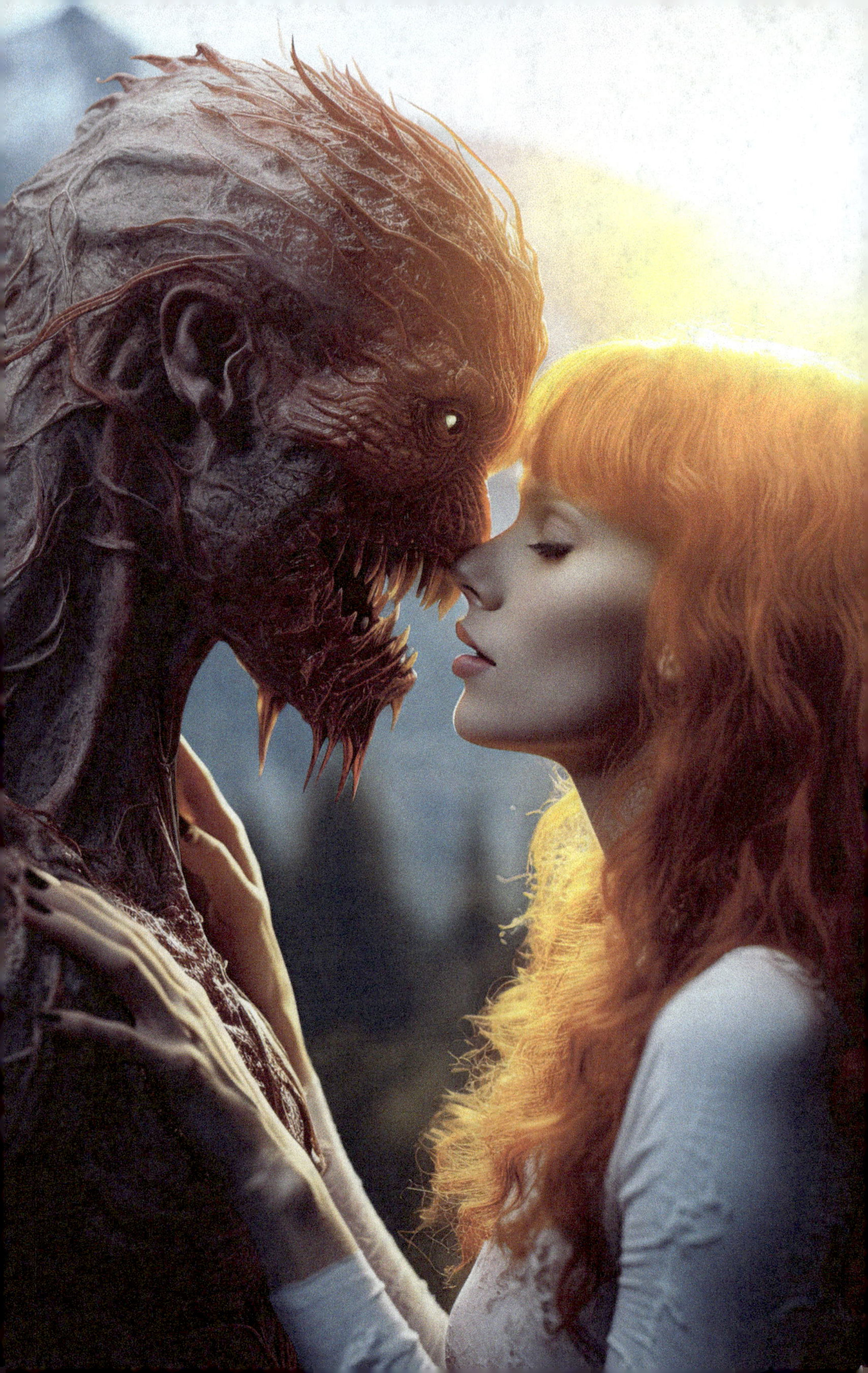

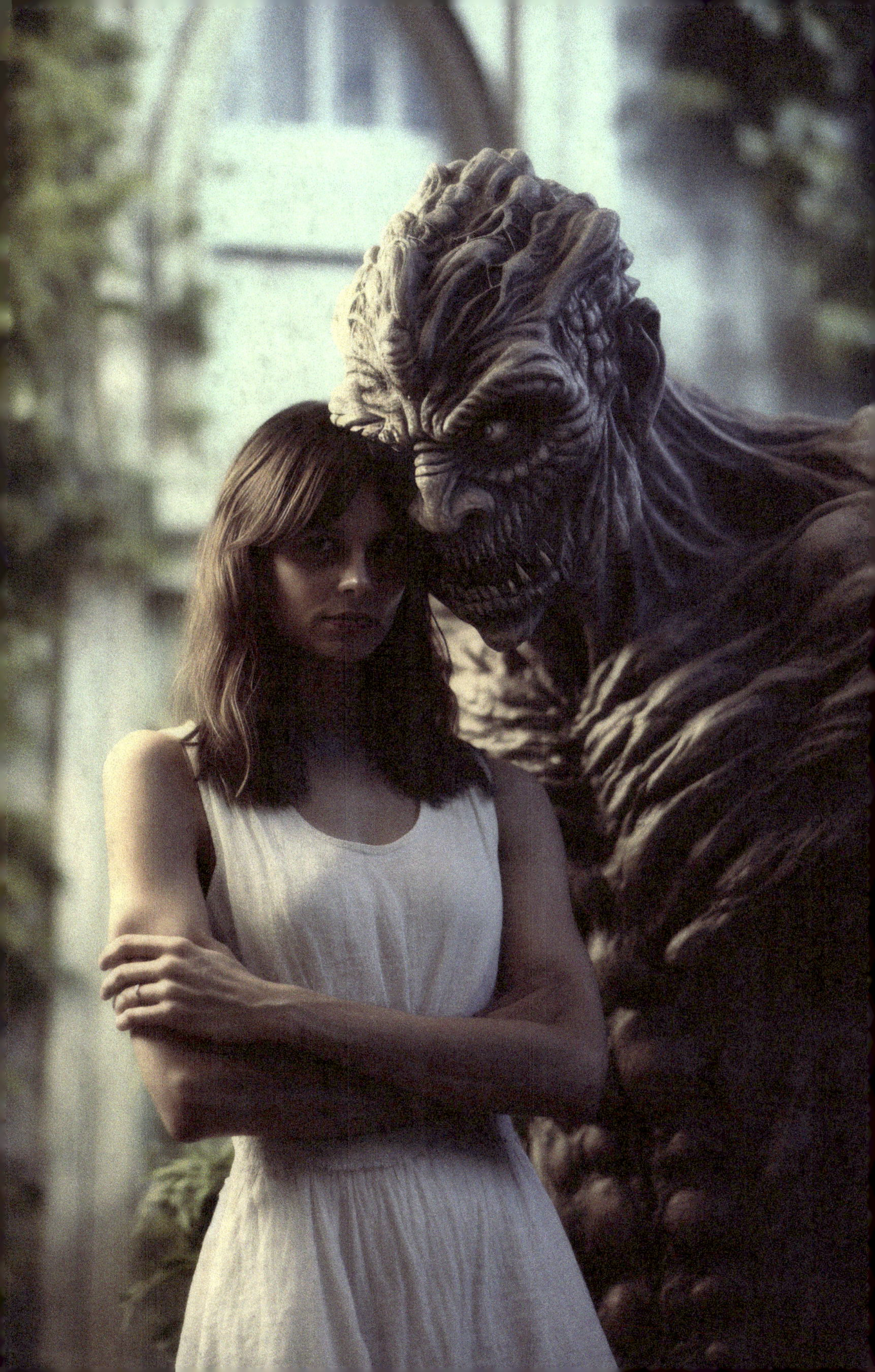

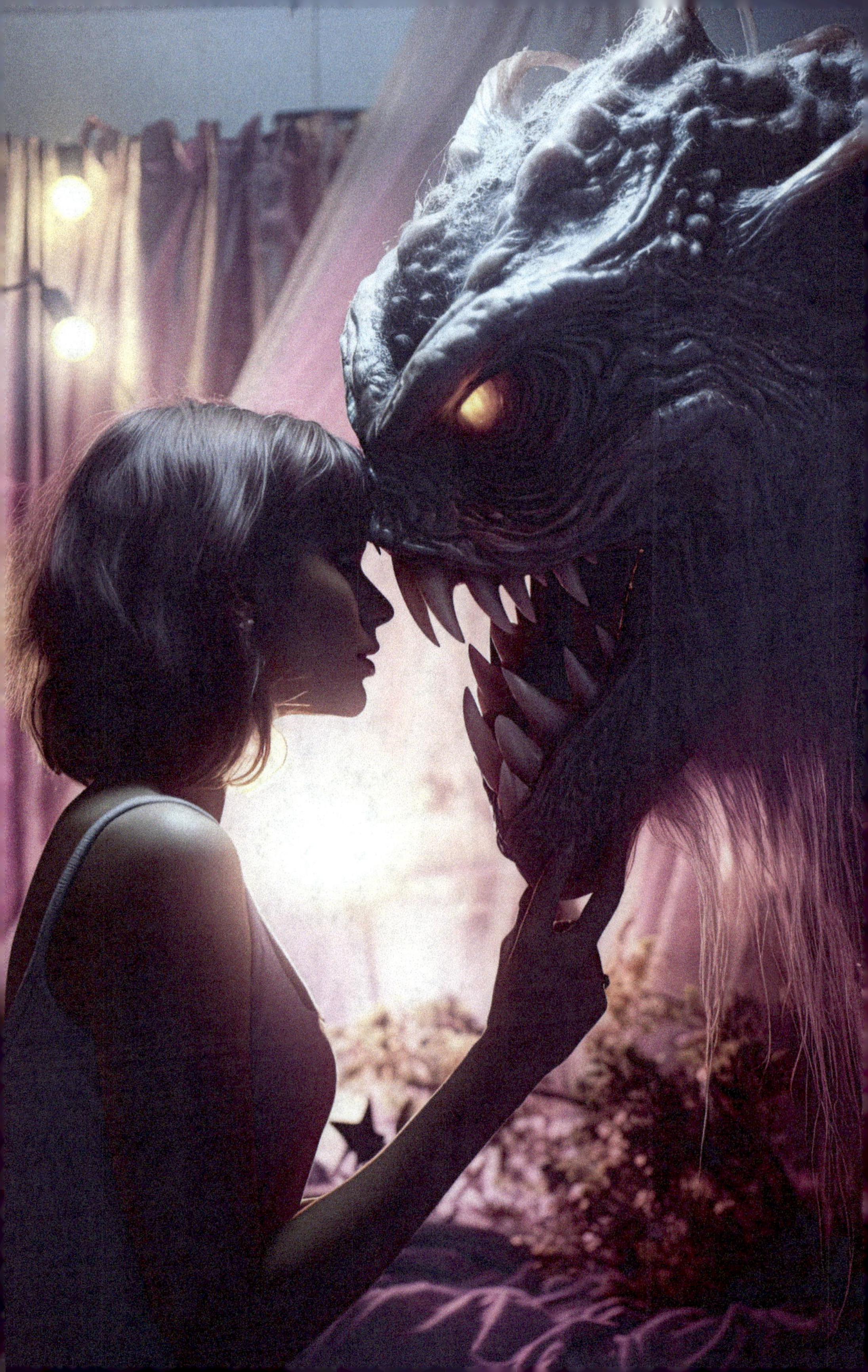

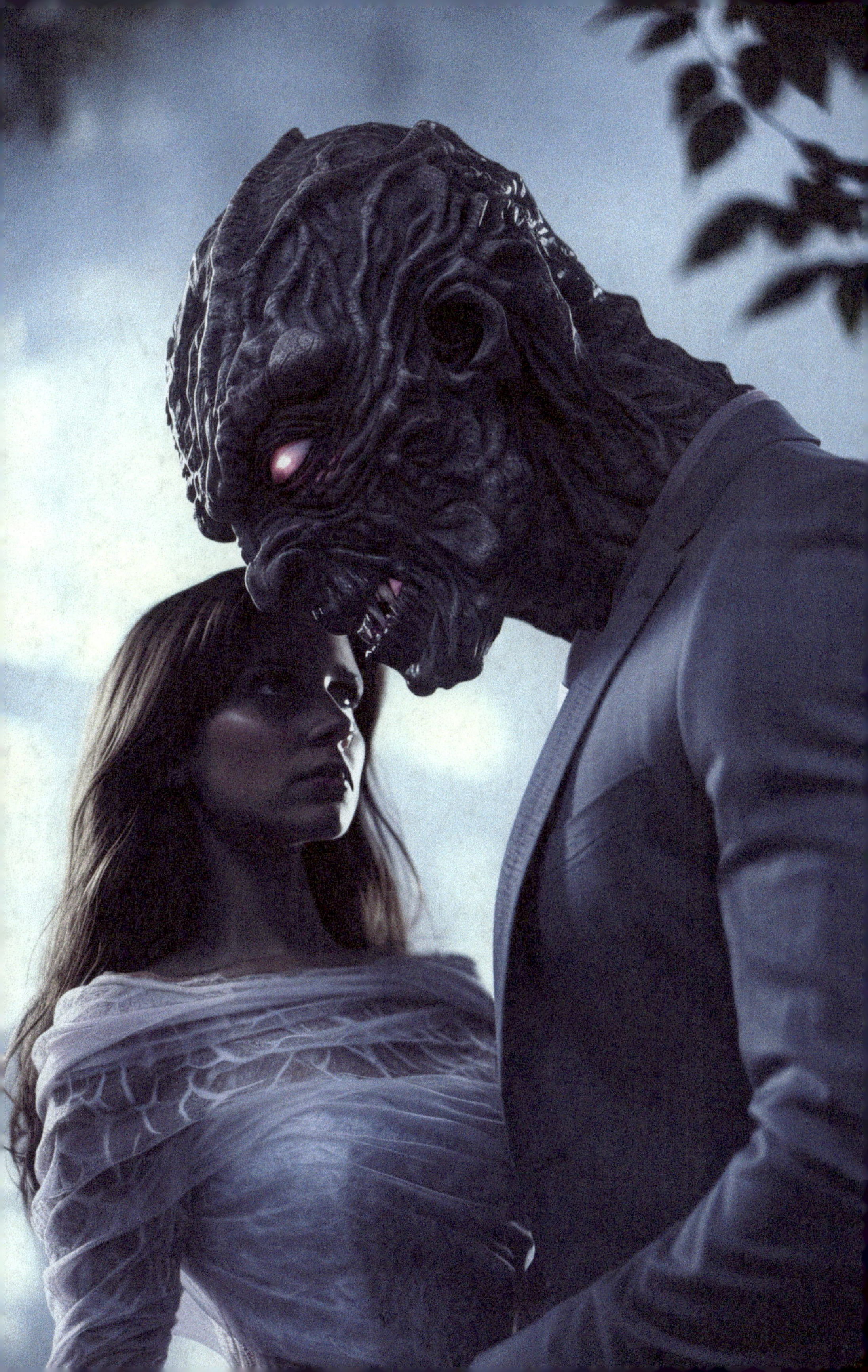

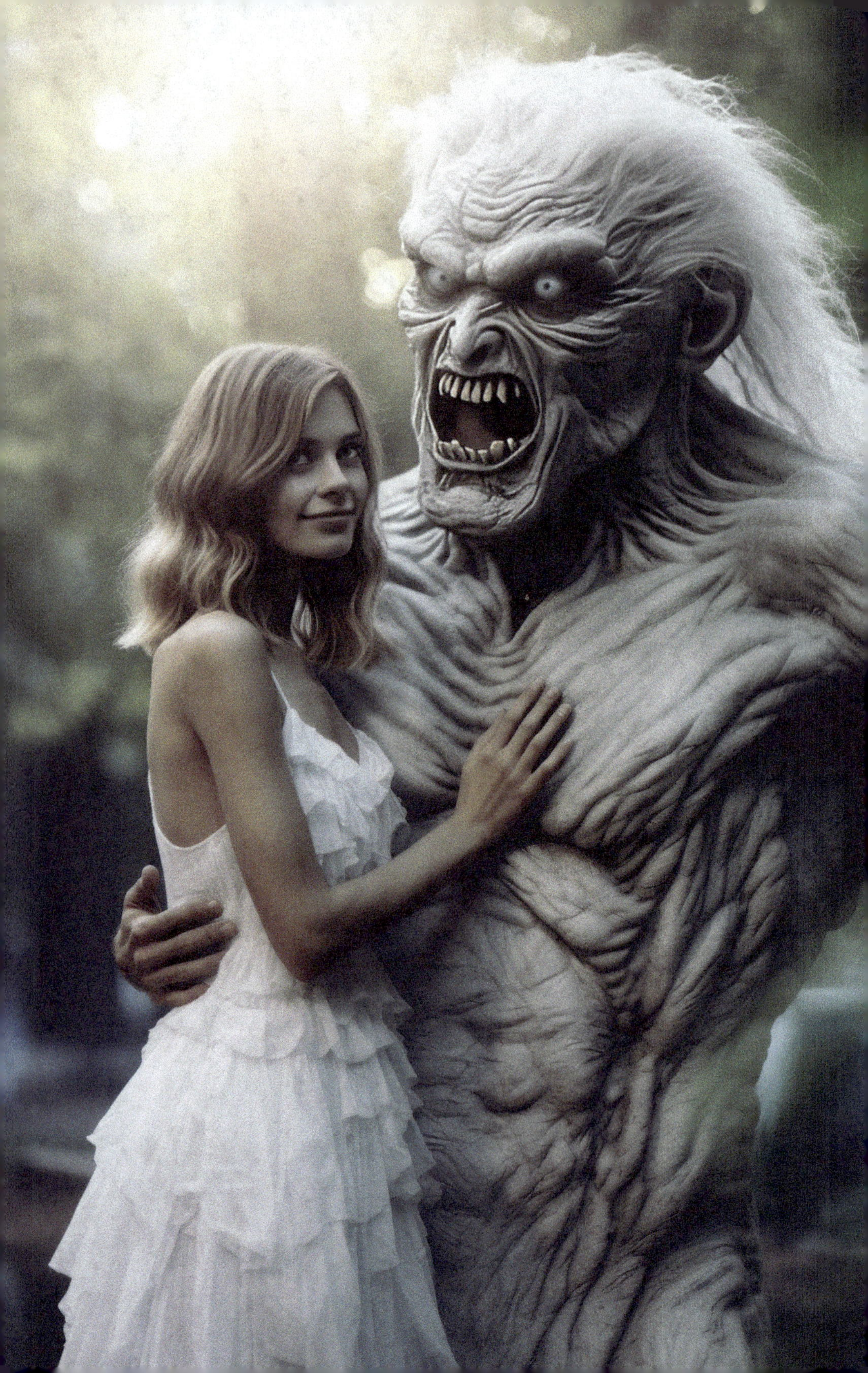

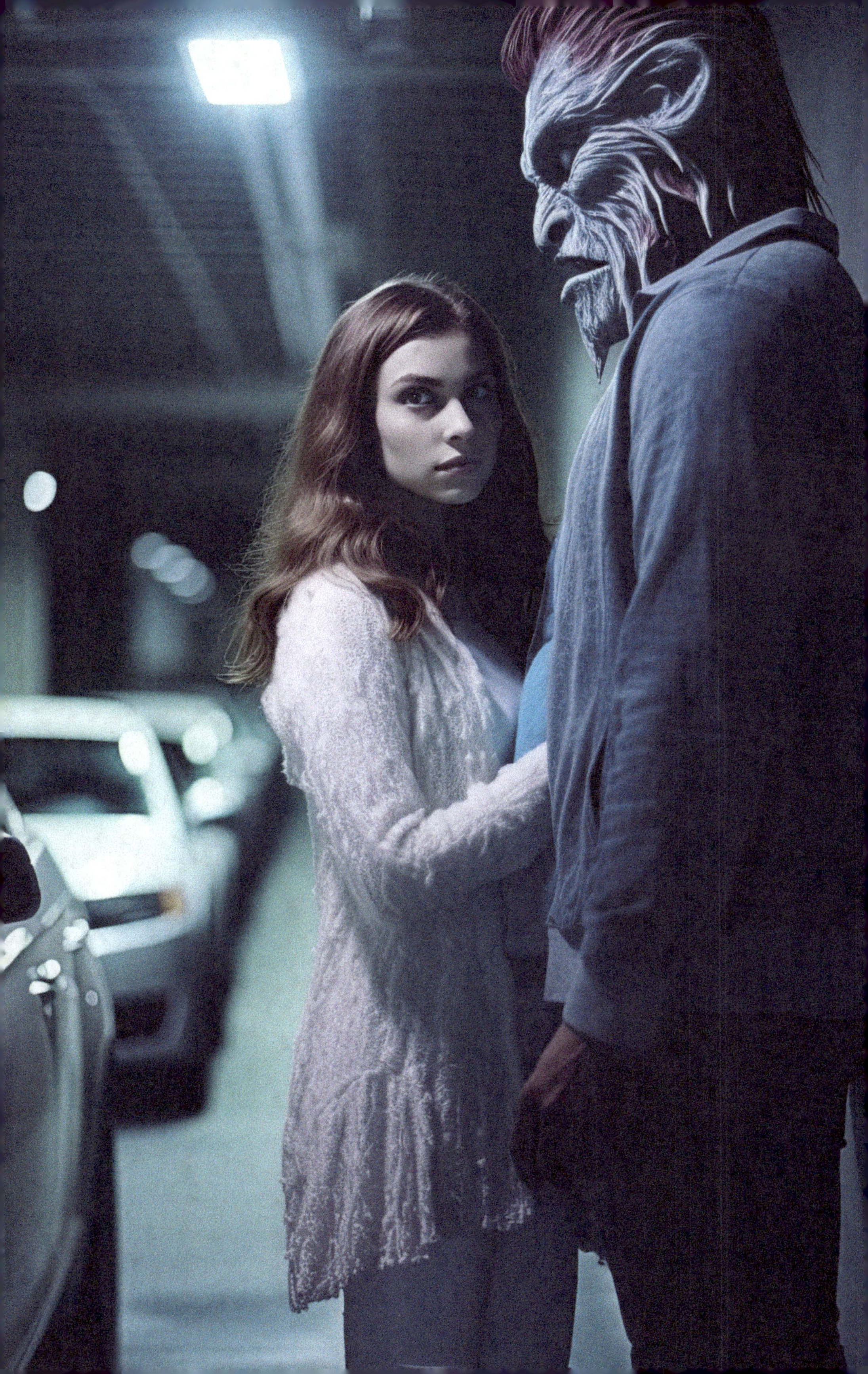

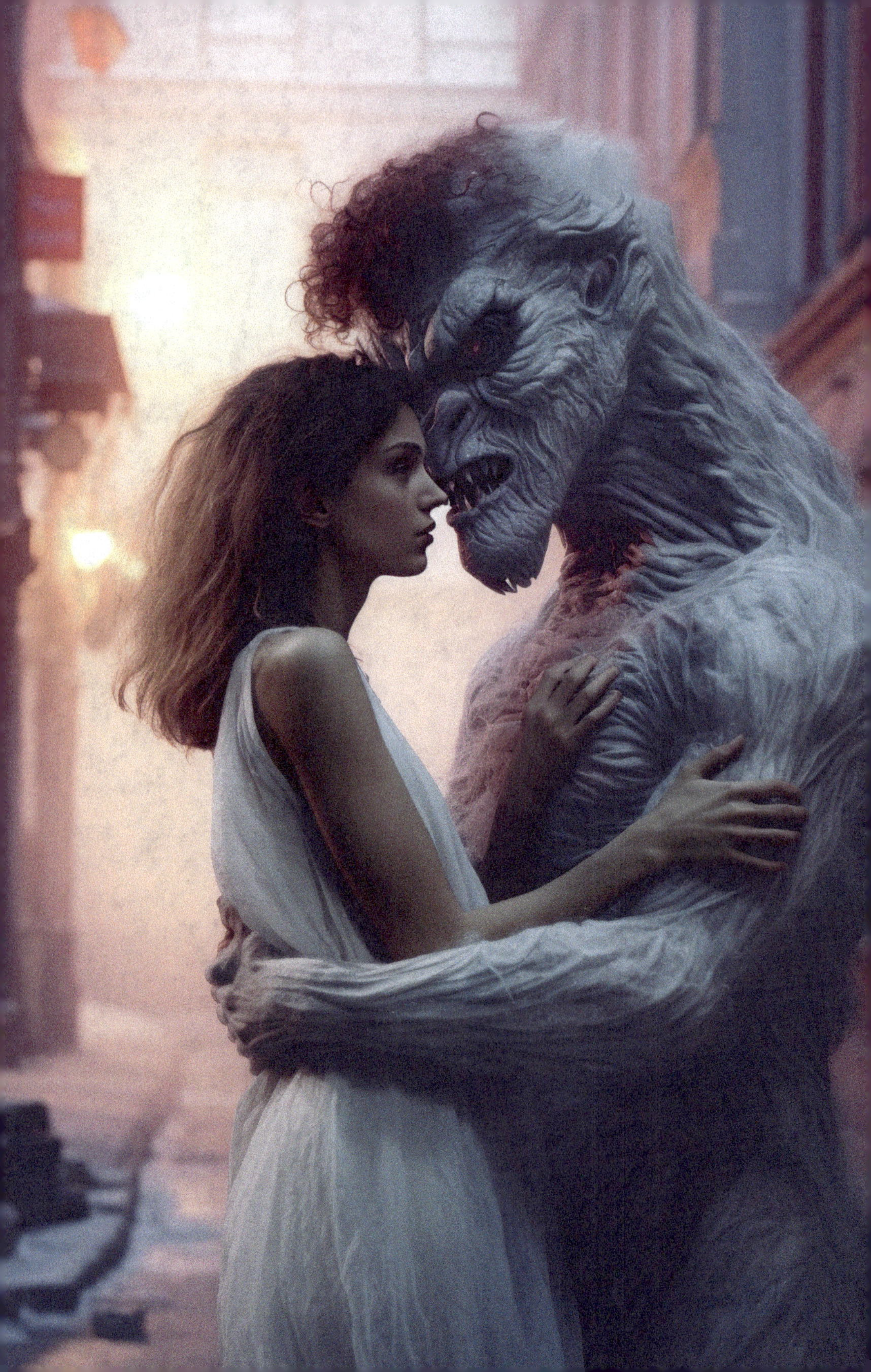

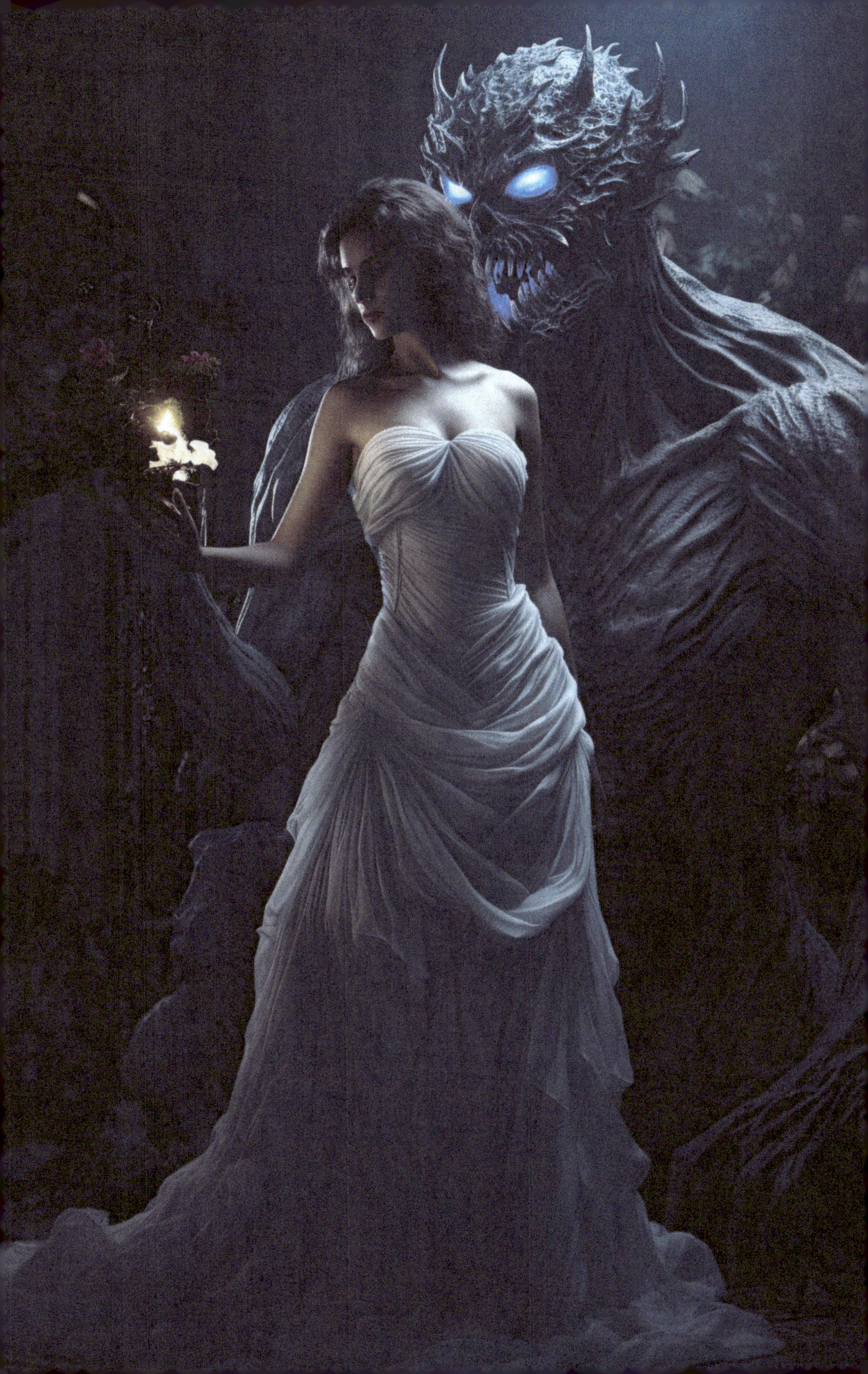

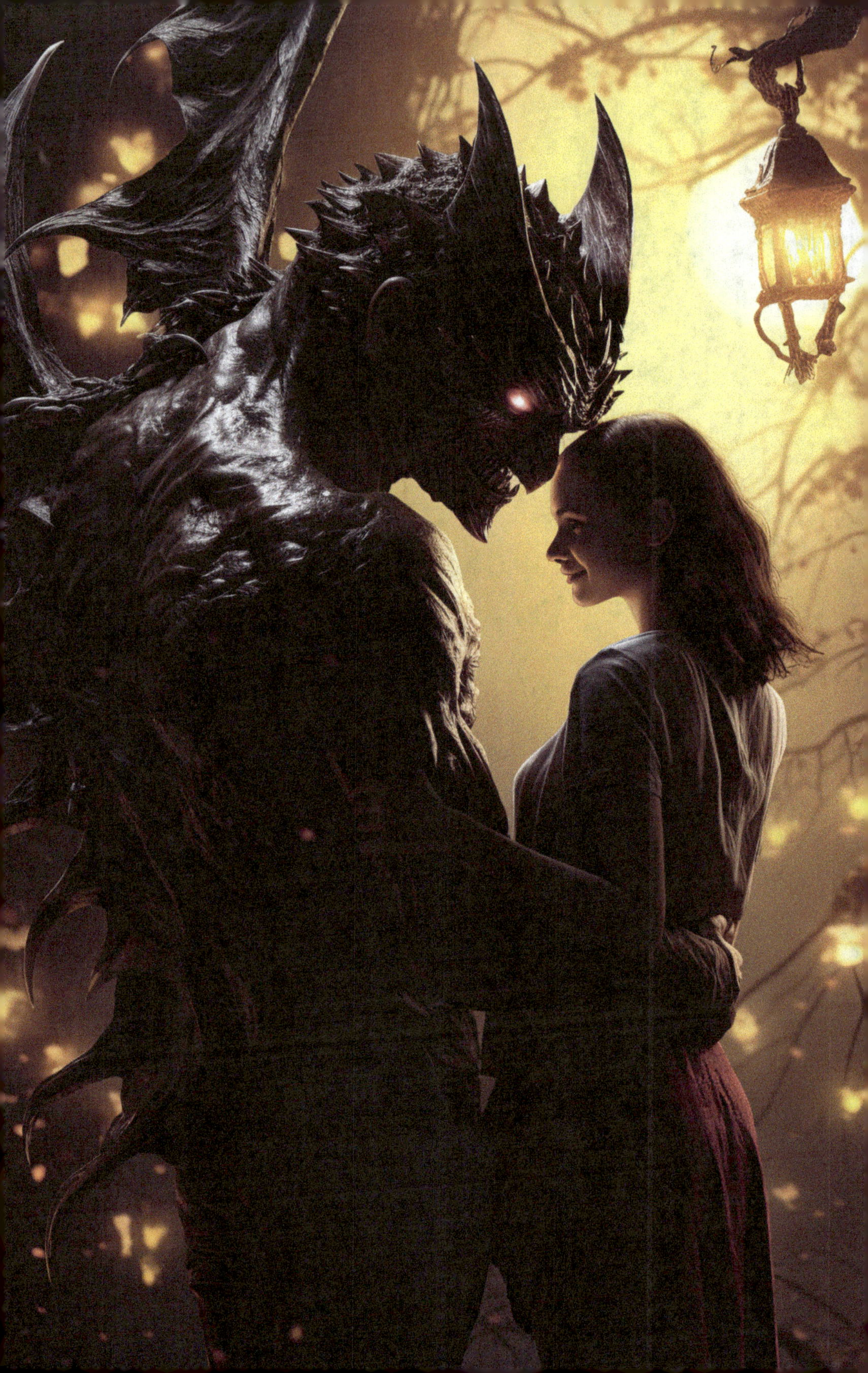

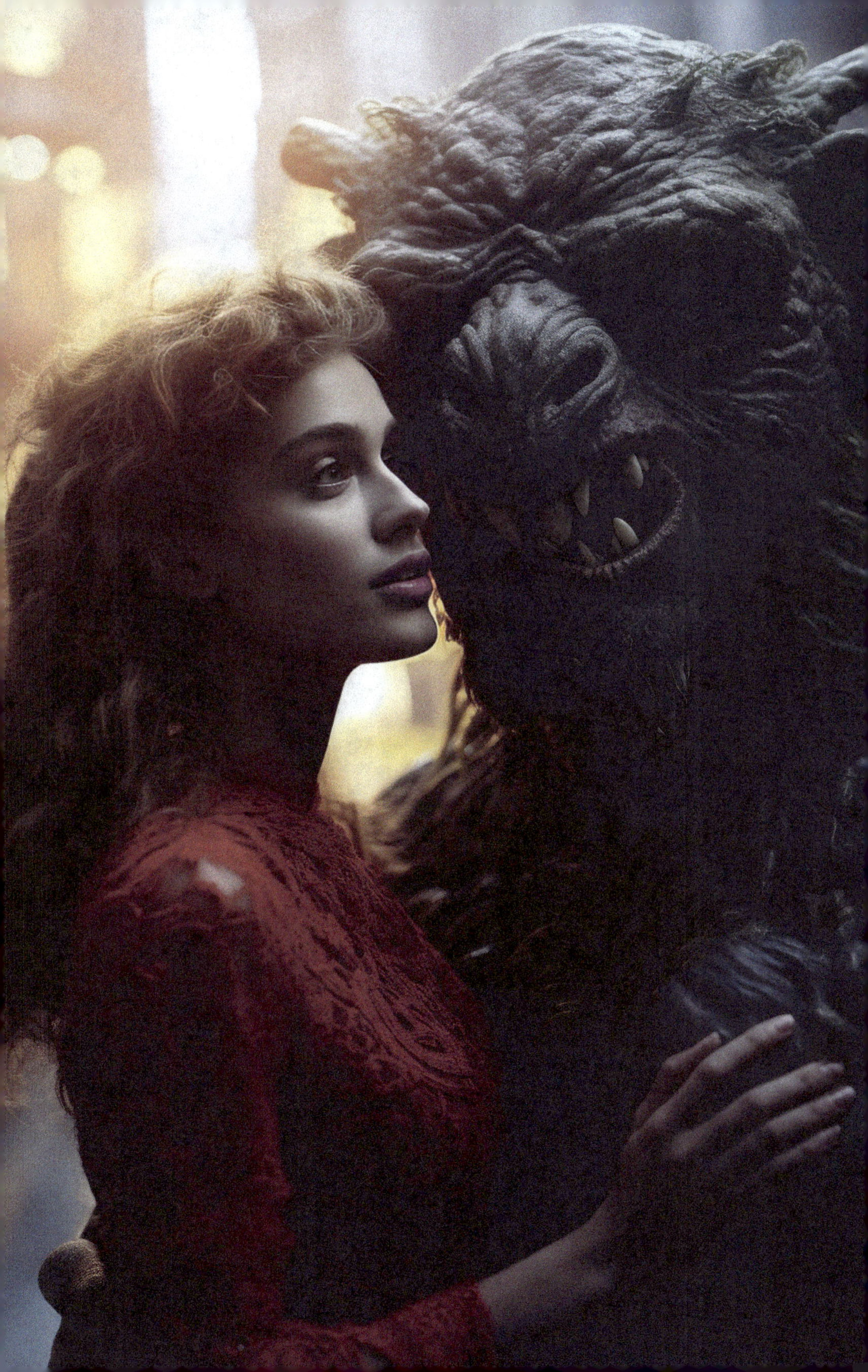

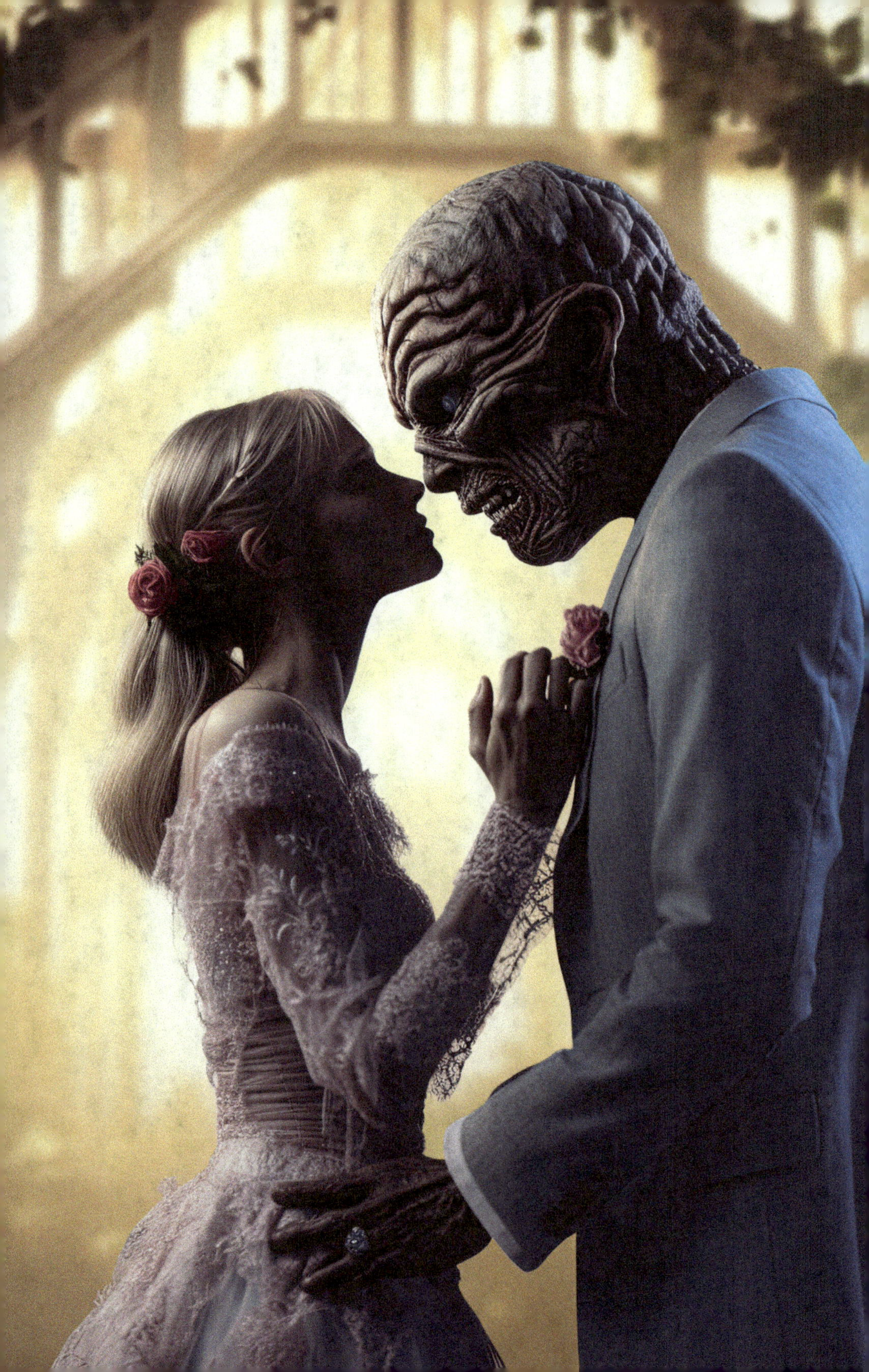

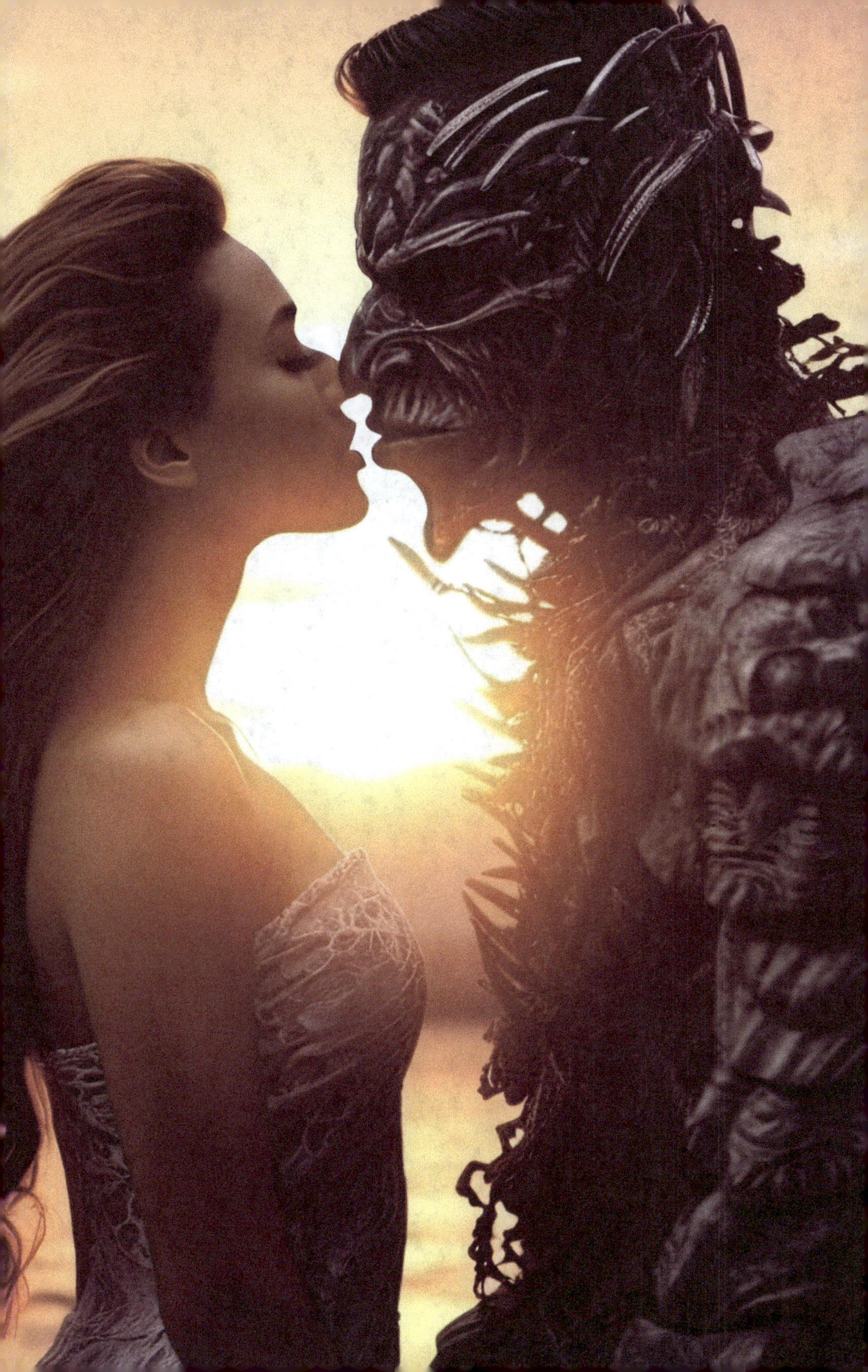

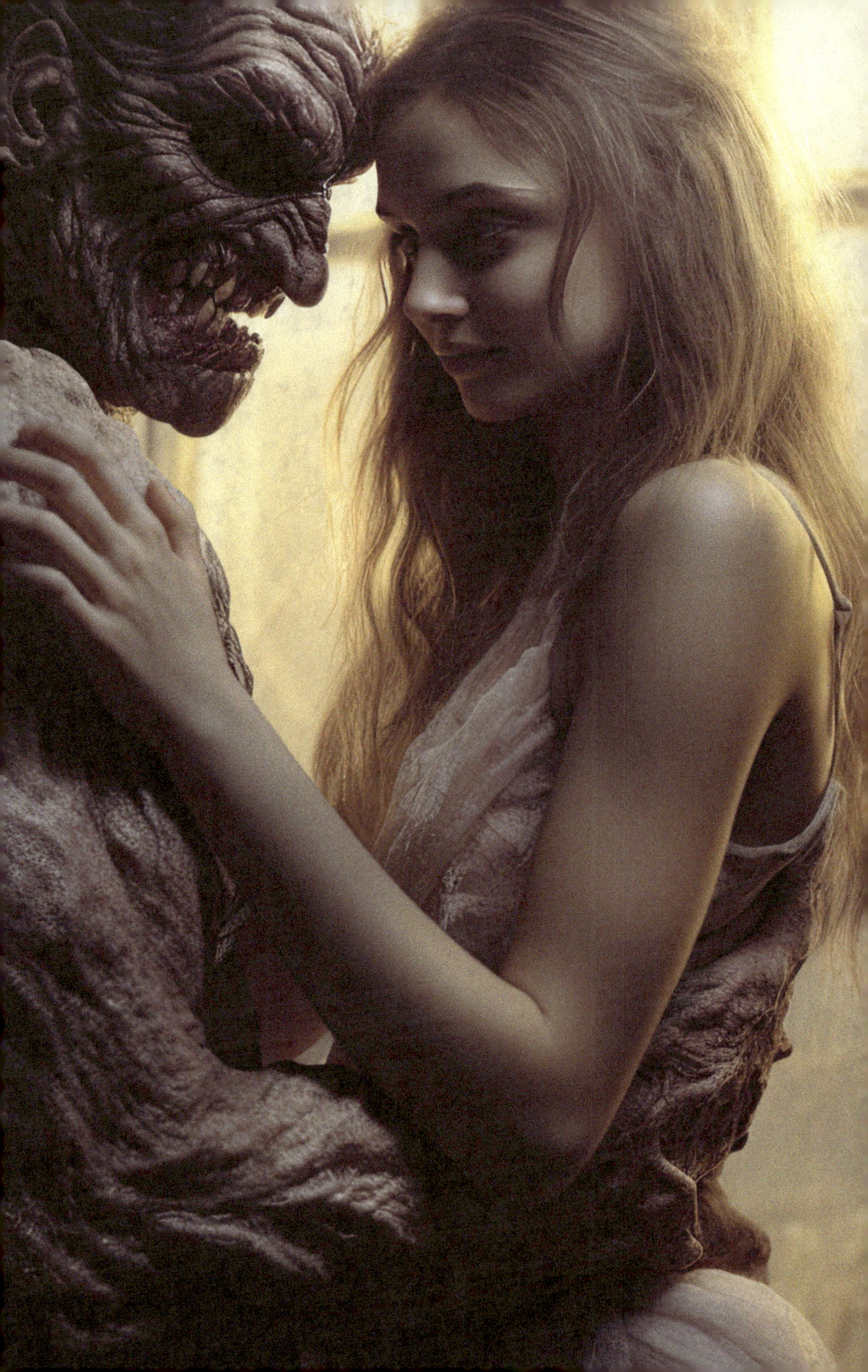

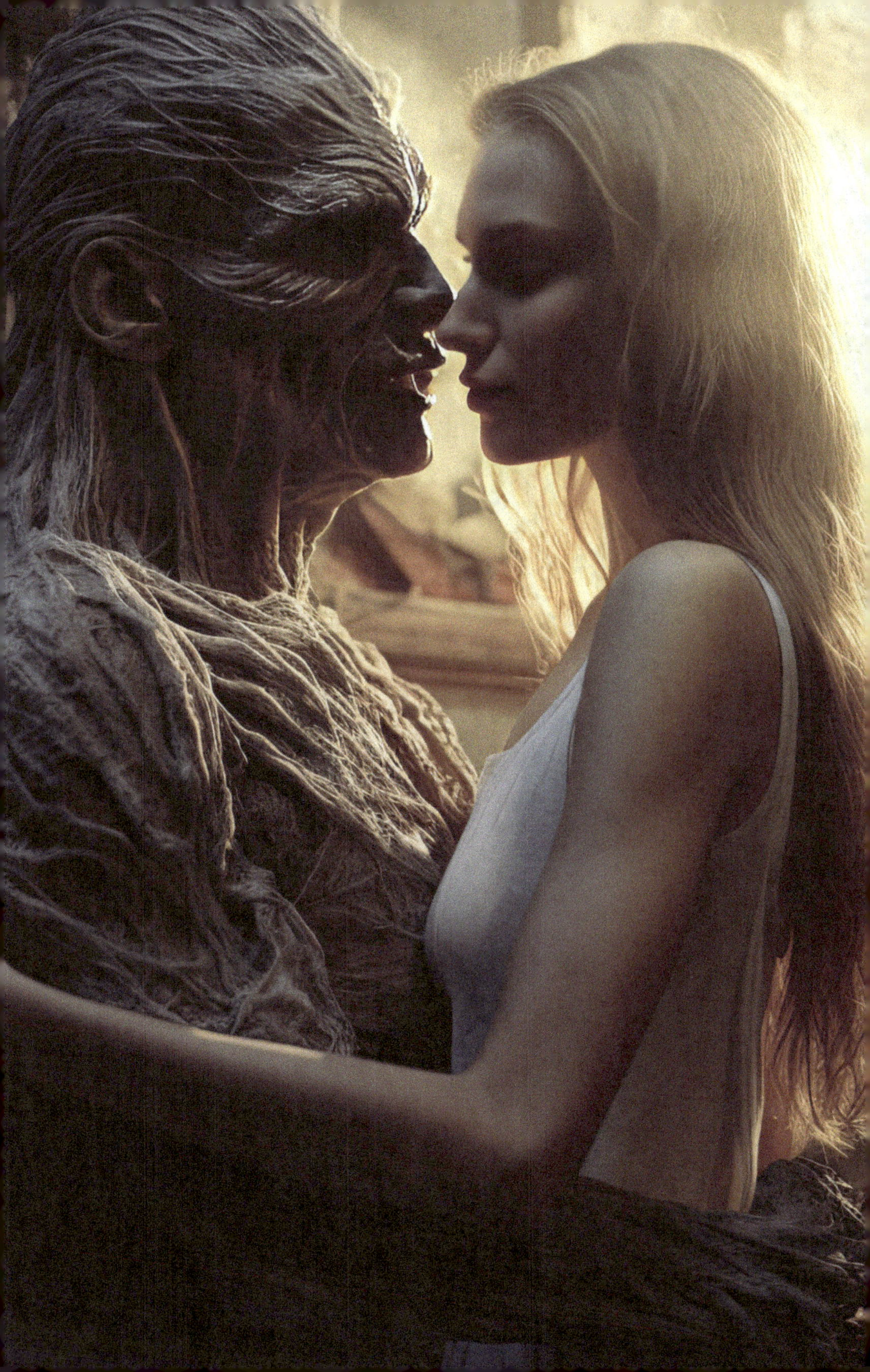

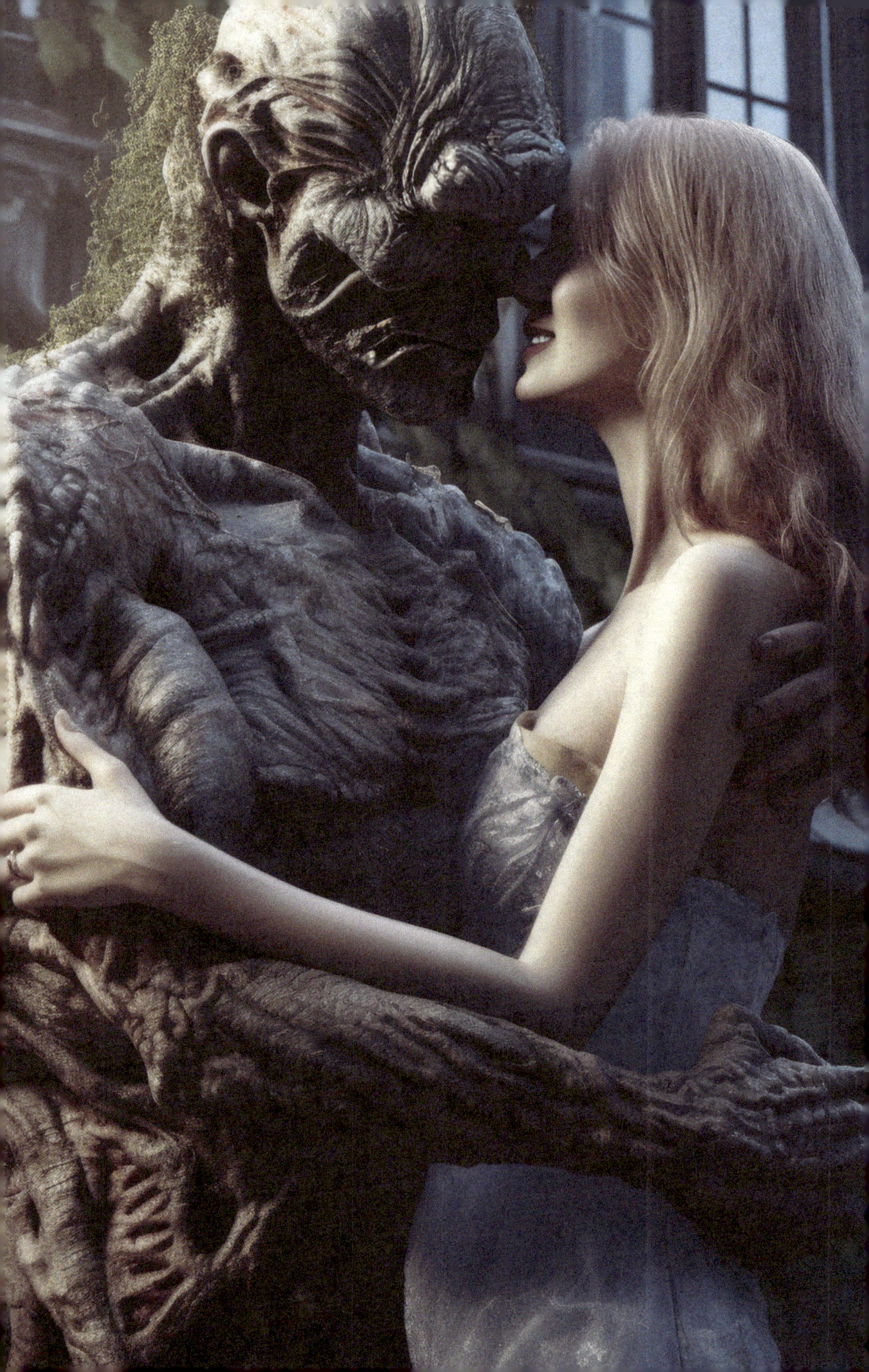

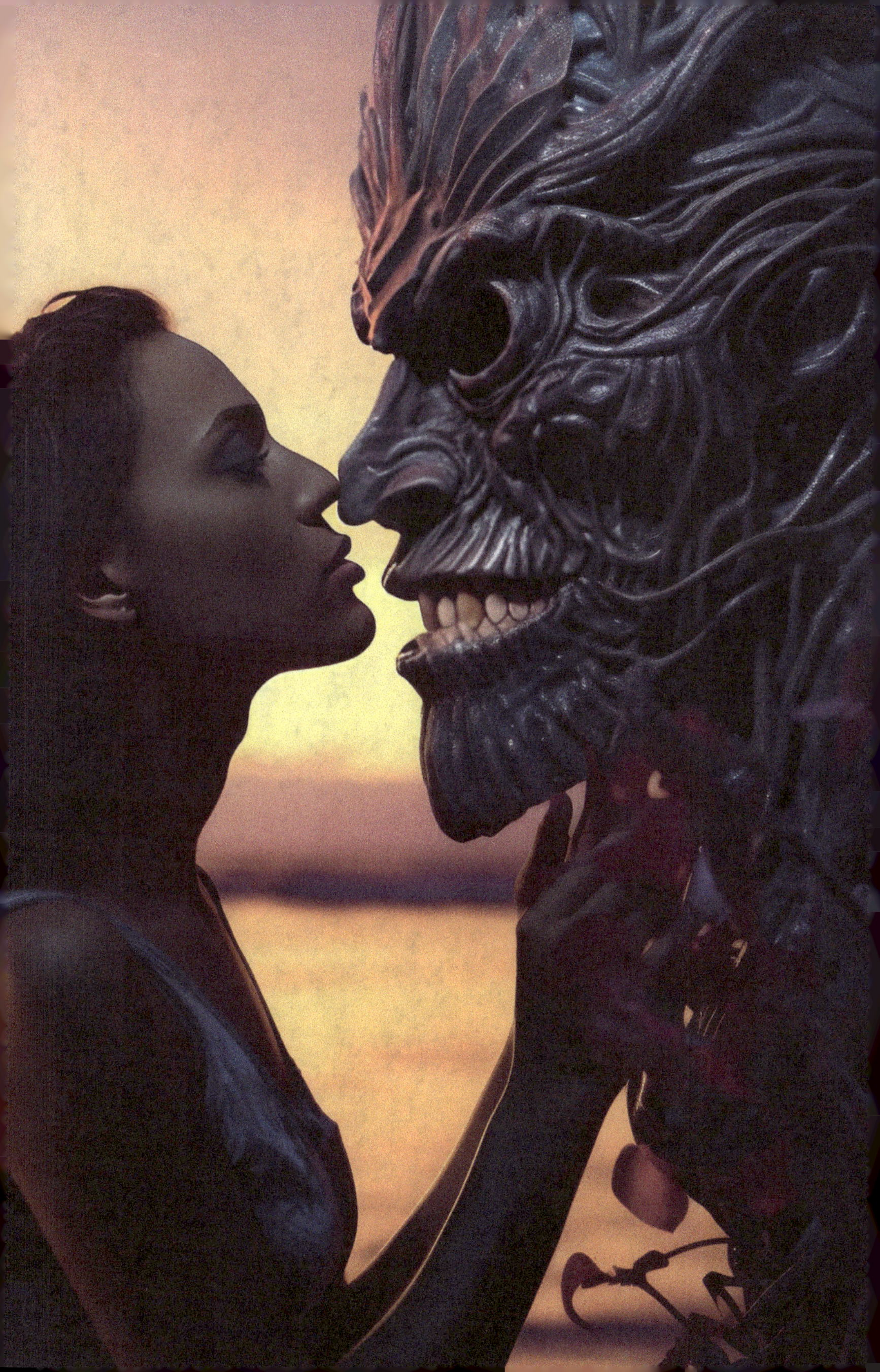

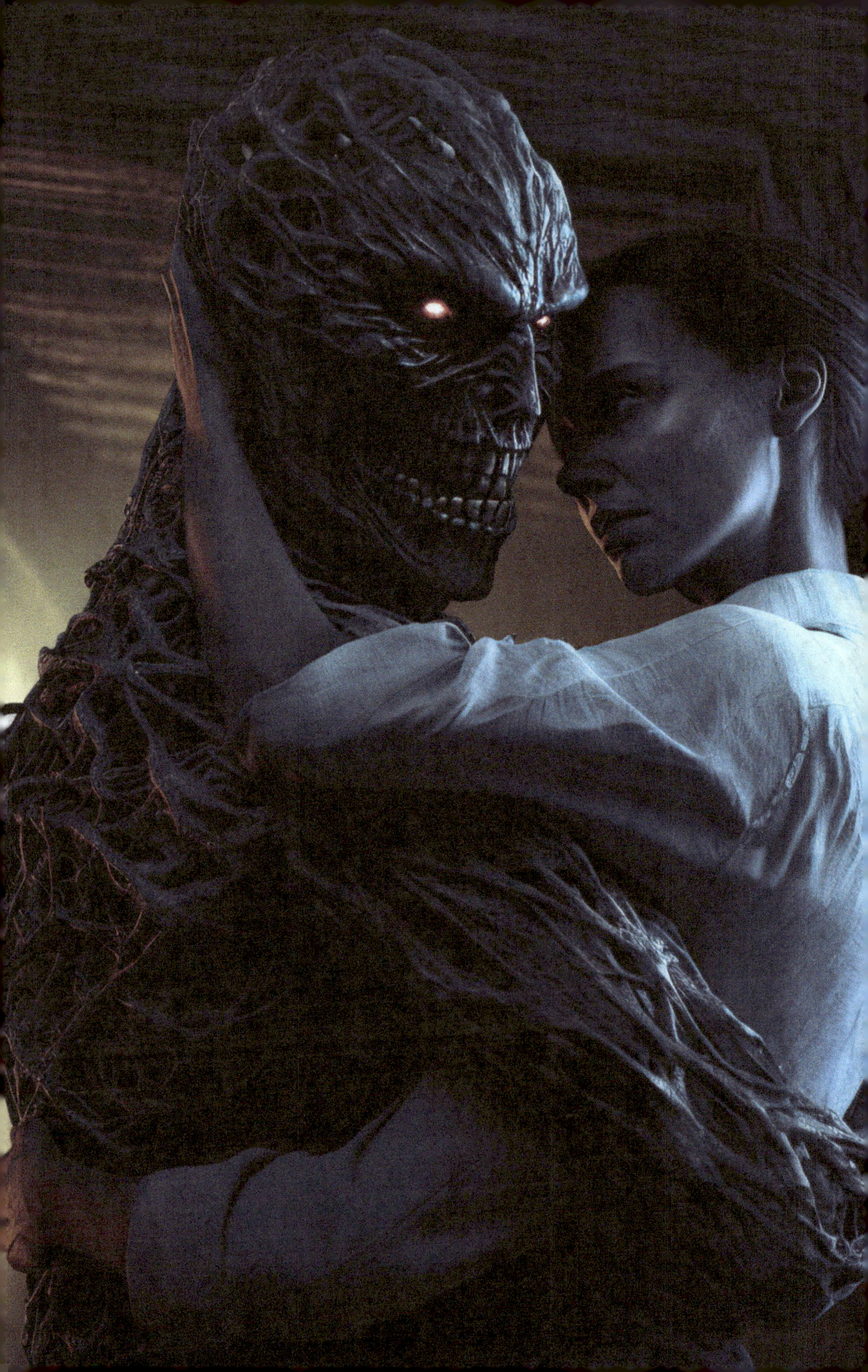

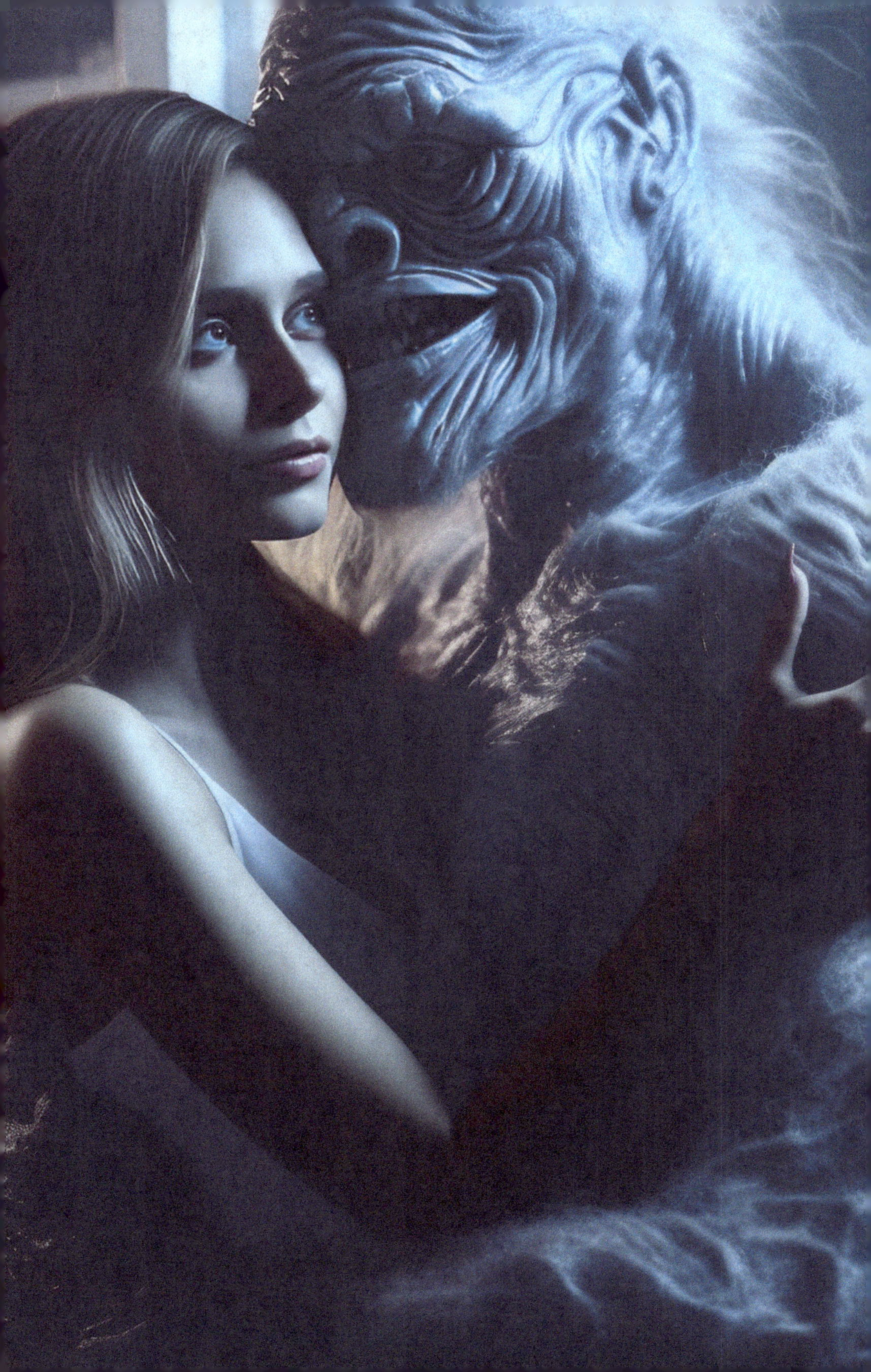

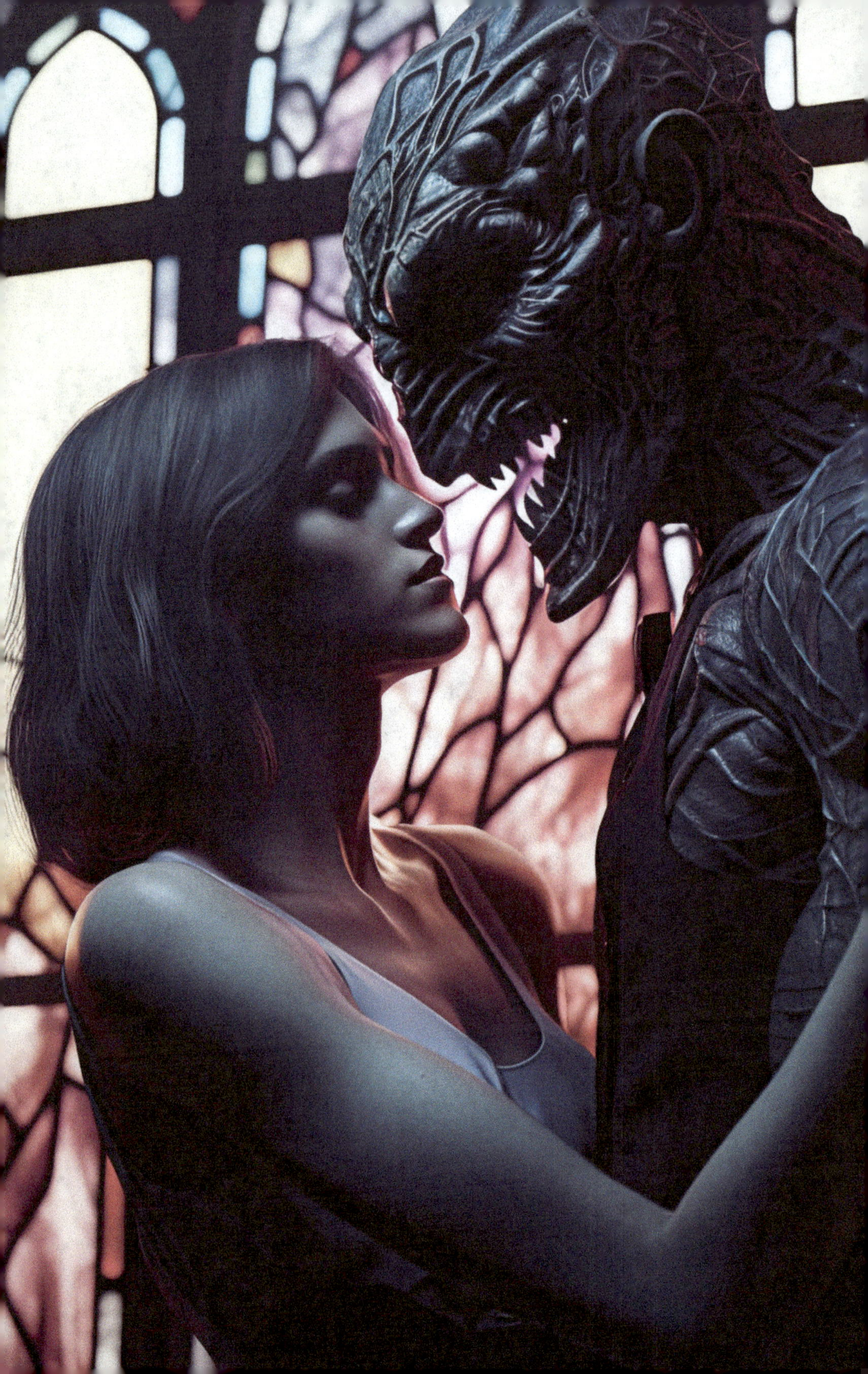

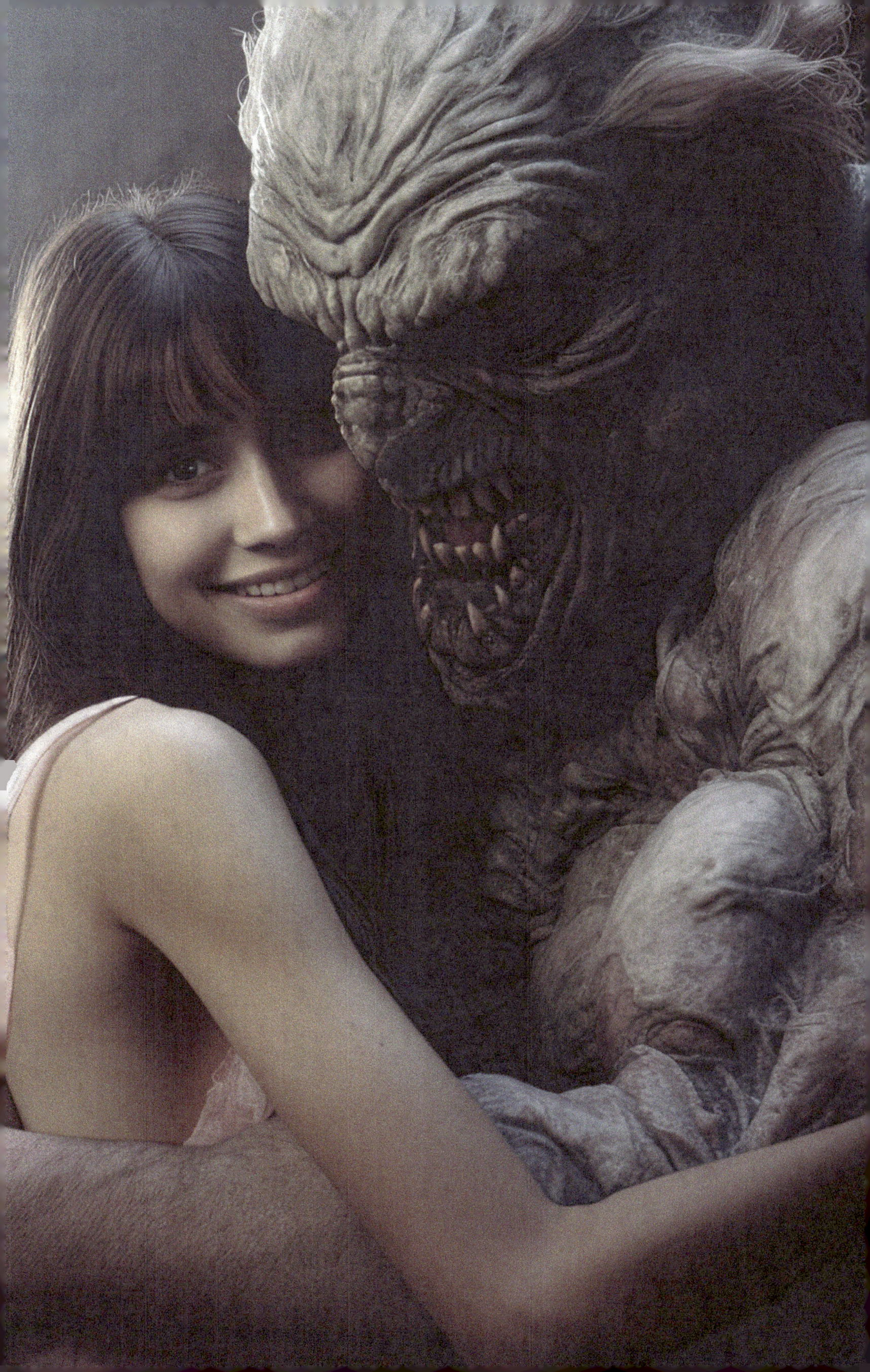

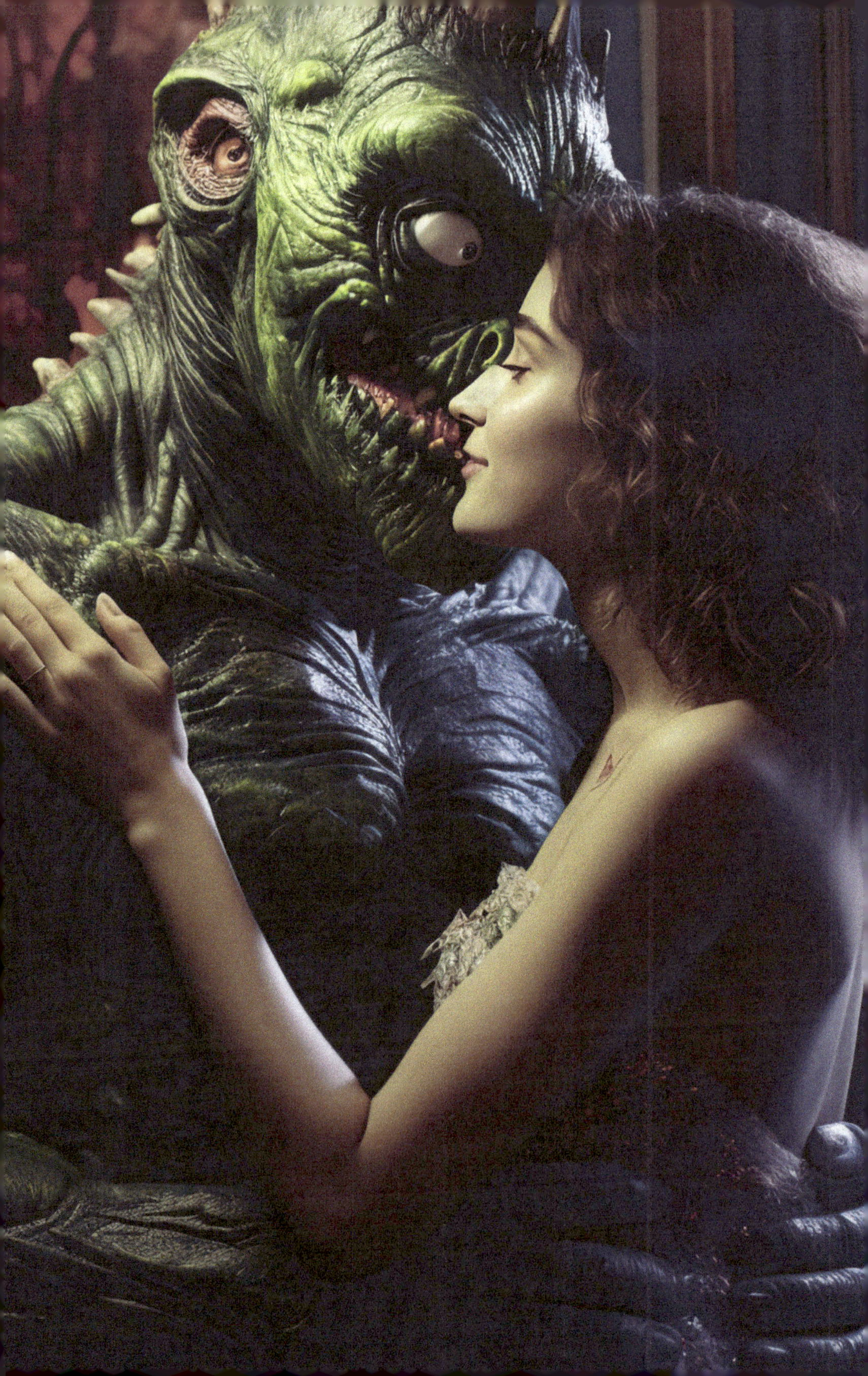

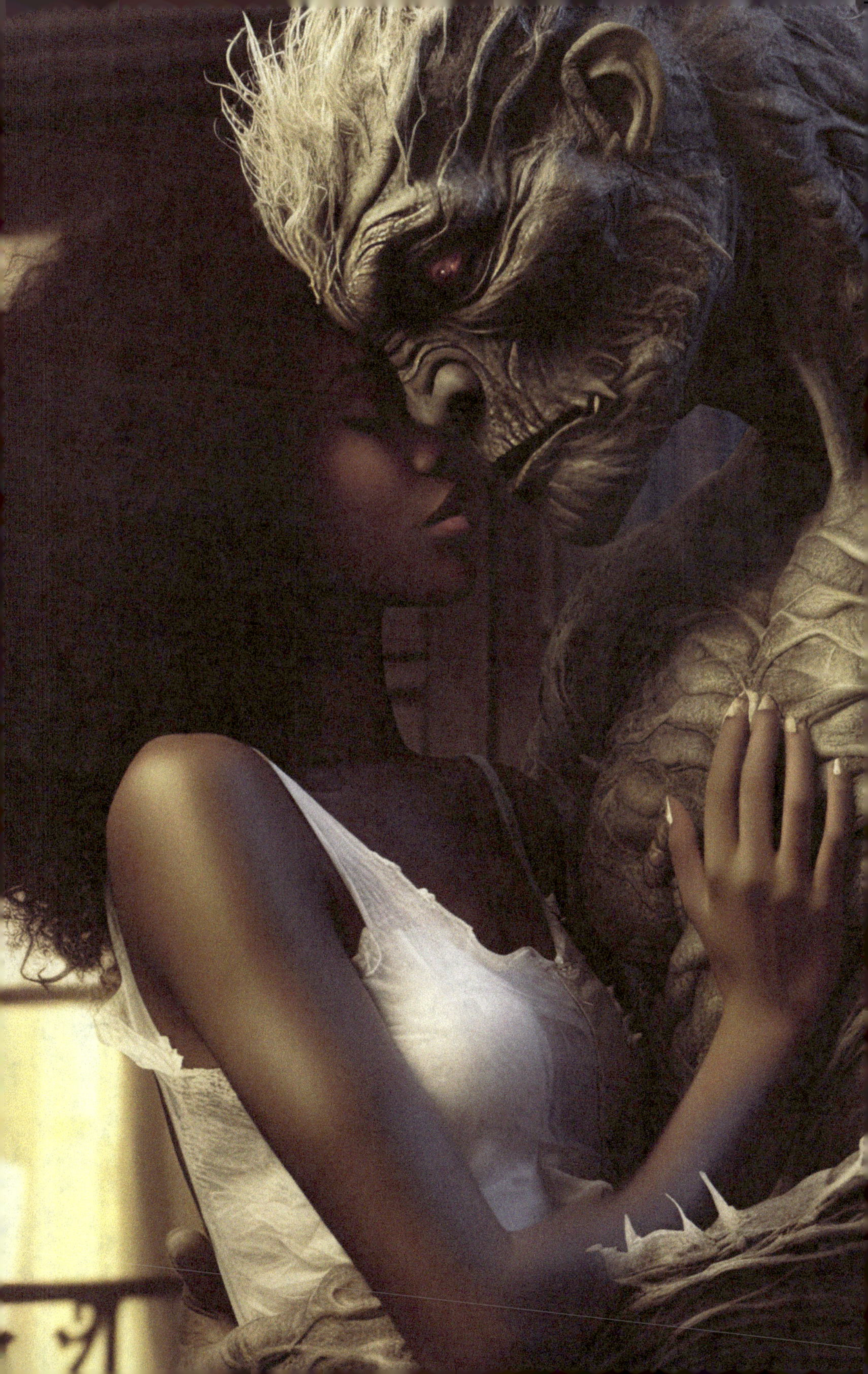

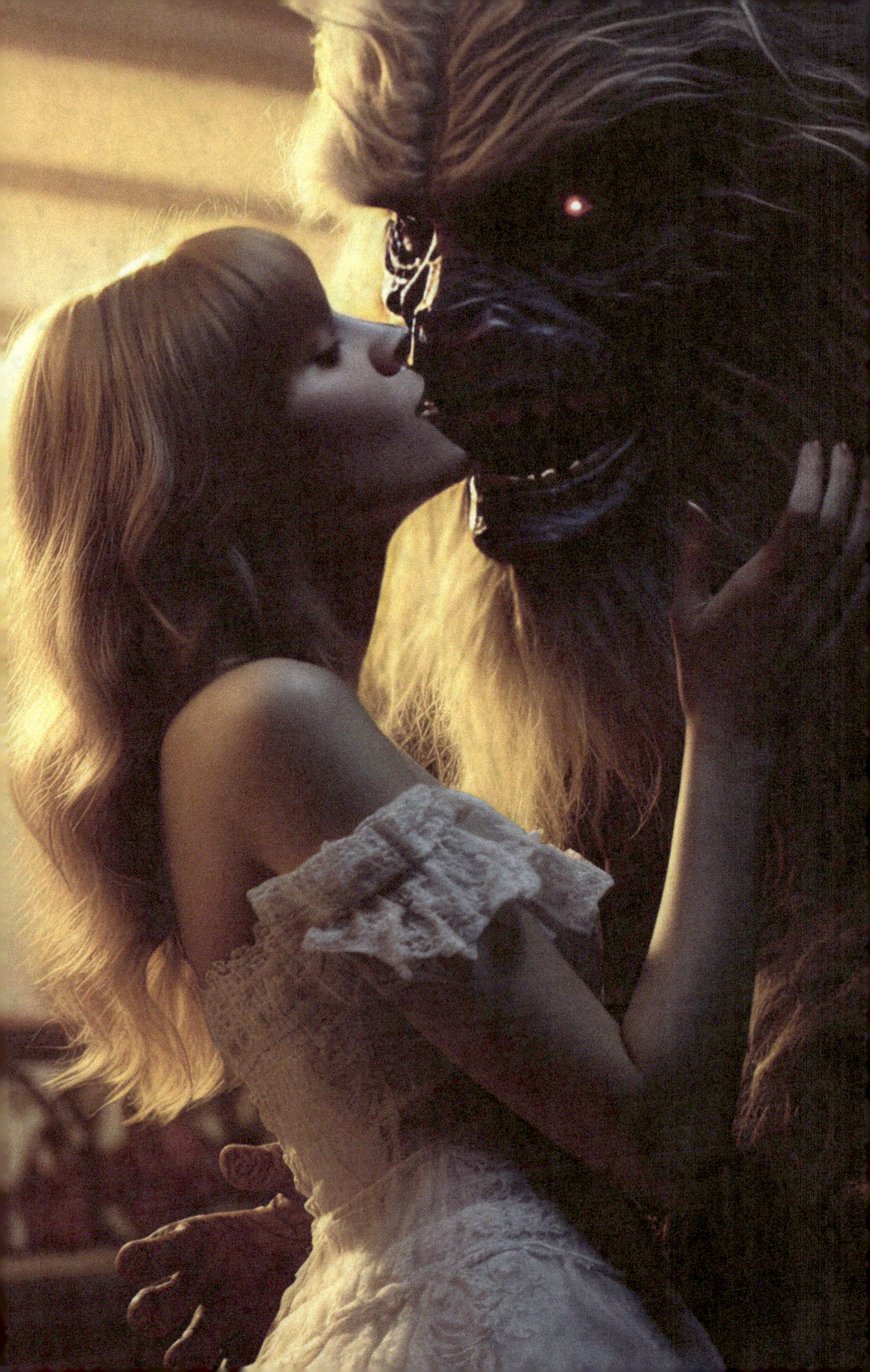

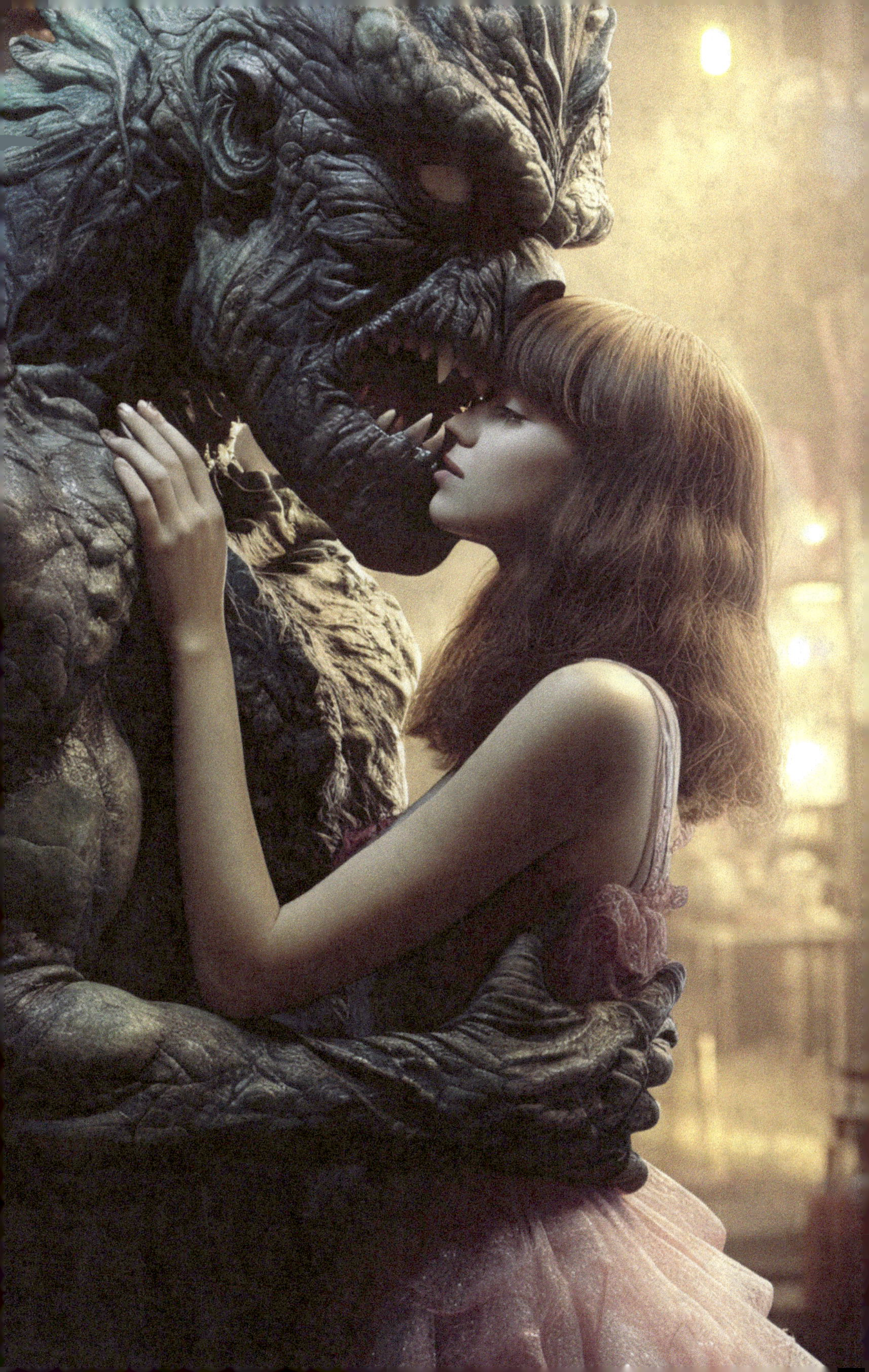

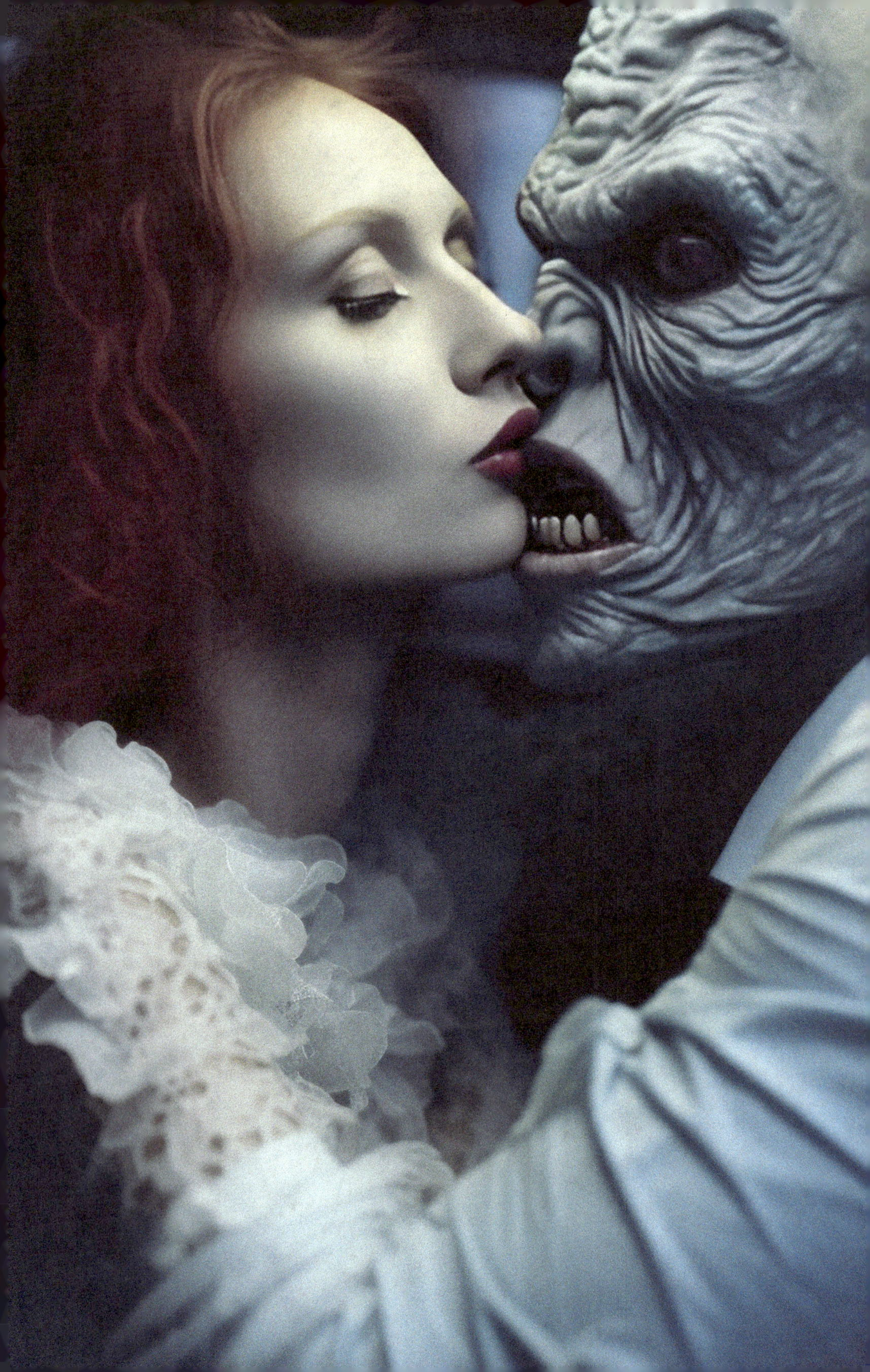

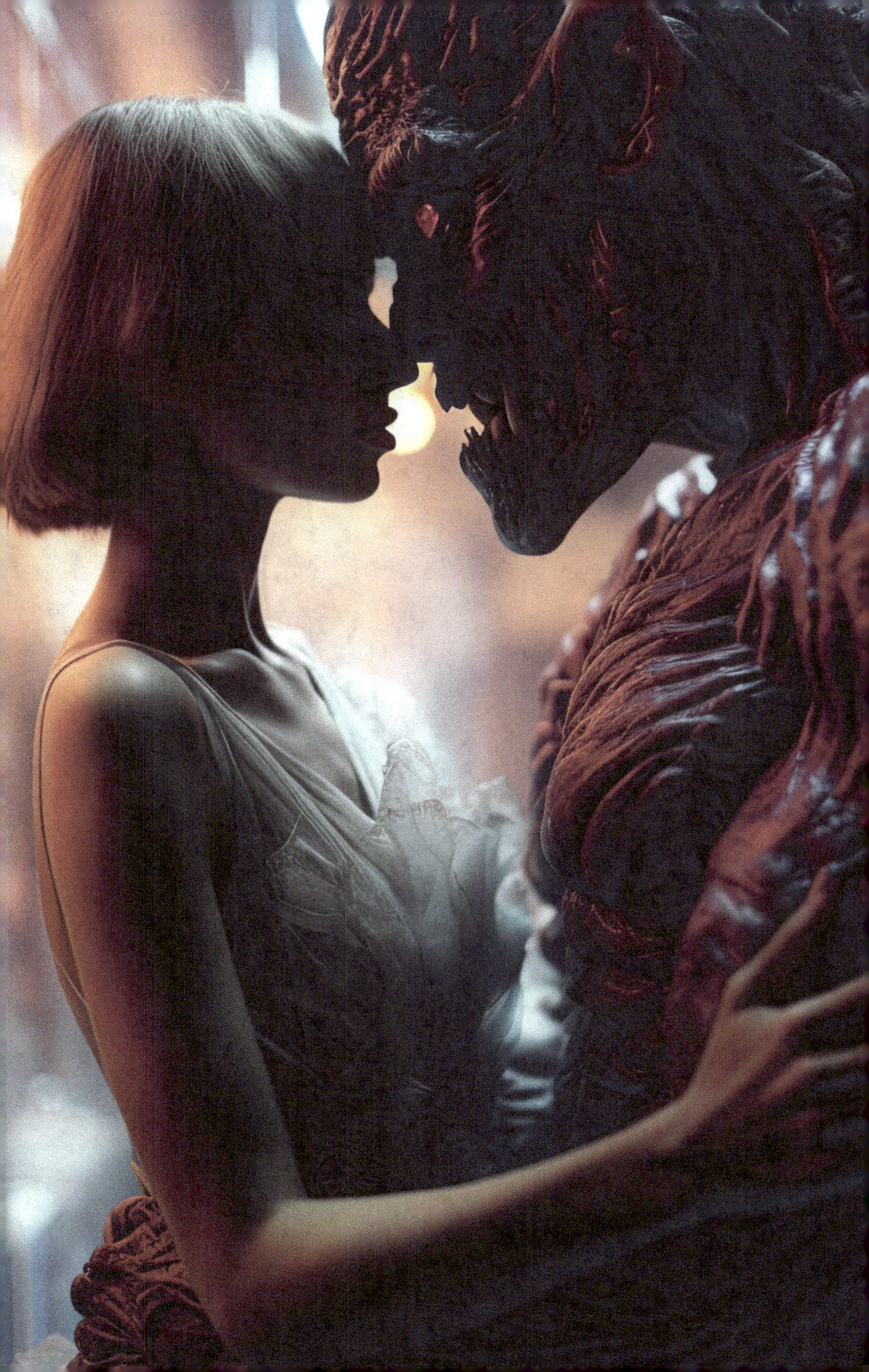

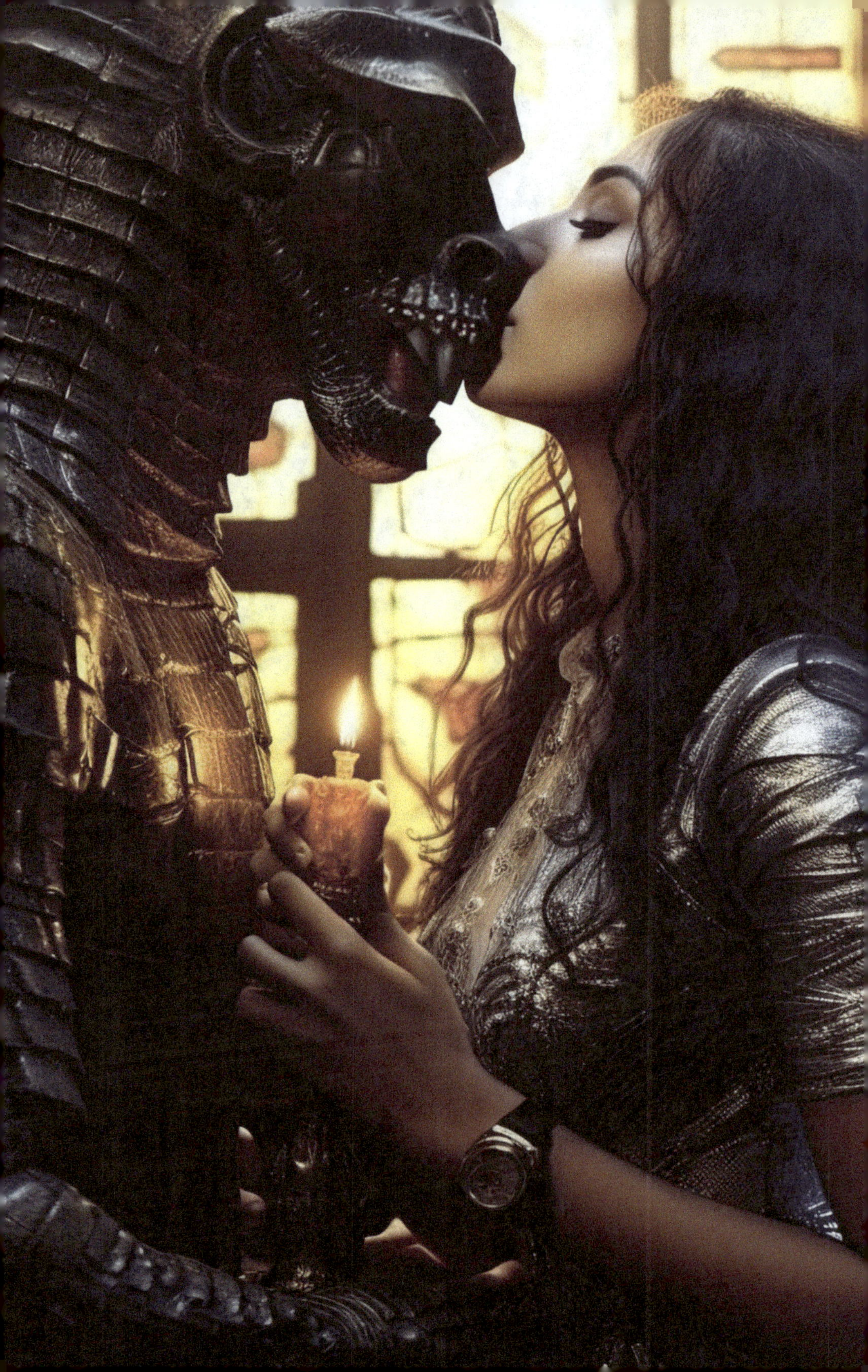